I0606071

BIBLE STORYBOOK

30 STORIES ILLUMINATING GOD'S LOVE AND REDEMPTION

BIBLE STORYBOOK

30 STORIES ILLUMINATING GOD'S LOVE AND REDEMPTION

Mary DeMuth and Sophie DeMuth

Salvation Poem™ PROJECT

Visit Tyndale's website for kids at tyndale.com/kids.

Learn more about Salvation Poem Project at salvationpoem.com. Learn more about *Light of the World* at lightoftheworld.com.

Light of the World Bible Storybook: 30 Stories Illuminating God's Love and Redemption

Illustrations by Kevin and Kristin Howdeshell, Kasie Lien, Katie Lee, Artiom Ceban, Jasmine Rogers, Francisco Anduiza, Nina Kwon, Claudia Corrales, Laura Correal, Chiu Yi, Leichen Wagner, Andres Corretje, Darnell Johnson, David and Staci Larson.

Cover design by Darnell Johnson.

Interior design by Josh Meyer and Darnell Johnson.

Published in association with Mary DeMuth Literary, MaryDeMuthLiterary.com.

For manufacturing information regarding this product, please call 1-855-277-9400.

For information about special discounts for bulk purchases, please contact Tyndale House Publishers at csresponse@tyndale.com, or call 1-855-277-9400.

ISBN 979-8-4005-1506-4

Printed in China.

32 31 30 29 28 27 26

7 6 5 4 3 2 1

CONTENTS

INTRODUCTION: WHEN I MET THE LIGHT

How the Darkness Started and How the Light Stepped in

Hi, I'm John—a close friend of Jesus. I spent time with him while he did many miracles, fed lots of people, and walked on water. There are so many things Jesus did and said that hundreds of thousands of books could not hold them all.

Today, I want to tell you a story about Jesus.

One day when we were together in the Temple (God's house), Jesus told me and my friends, "I am the Light of the World."

To be honest, life before I met Jesus was hard—dark, even. My nation, Israel, was waiting for God to help them, but it seemed like he did not care at all. For centuries, God had been silent. No prophets. No miracles. No voice of God. Not only that, but Rome, a powerful and cruel nation, had taken over and terrified us. We were not free, and we needed a Savior.

When Jesus said he was the Light, I was so happy. Could it be that God was finally going to come to us and do something? The ancient writings from God reminded me that he always cares for his people and would someday visit us to deliver us.

Jesus kept talking. "If you follow me, you won't have to walk in darkness, because you will have the light that leads to life."

What does he mean? I wondered.

On that day in the Temple, I didn't quite know, but now I understand because of another story the Bible tells.

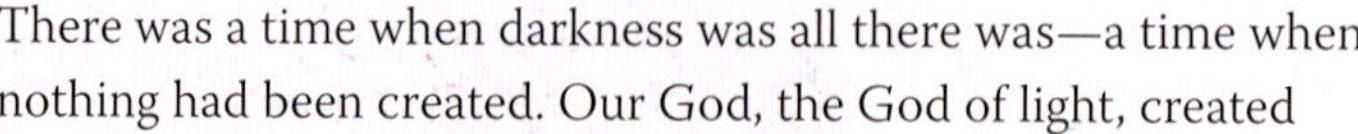

There was a time when darkness was all there was—a time when nothing had been created. Our God, the God of light, created light—and he also made everything we see. He made a beautiful garden, and in that place, he made a man and a woman. God longed for friendship with them, so every day **Adam, Eve, and God walked together in the cool of the day, and all was light.**

Until everything fell apart. **A sneaky snake convinced the couple to disobey God, and all that had once been happy turned to sadness. Light flickered out.**

But God's great rescue plan was already in motion. He made promises to a new nation, Israel, that he would be their God and they would be his people. He chose people like Noah, Sarah, Moses, Ruth, and David and taught them about himself. This nation would tell the other nations about God's light and love so that everyone could live in his light.

But Israel couldn't hold up their part of the agreement. Instead of loving God and sharing his light with others, they chased after the darkness of other nations and suffered for it. Eventually Israel was taken away to another country. All seemed lost until a small band of Israelites returned to their home, rebuilt the Temple, and fixed the wall around the capital city, Jerusalem.

Even in that return, something was missing—God's presence. Darkness fell like a shadow over God's people. And they longed for light.

That's why I was so excited when I heard that Jesus was the light. He was God with skin on, visiting Israel *and* the whole wide world. He came to restore what had been lost when Adam and Eve disobeyed God. He lived a perfect life—can you imagine? And he gave his life willingly for me, for you, and for the whole big world. As God's Son, he died for us, then sprang to life again. Darkness could not hold Jesus in its grip.

I'm here to help you understand this powerful story of light. God has always been our light, and he loves to walk through the darkness with people who are scared, hurting, or alone. Whether you're reading stories about Jesus from before he was born, while he lived, or after he rose and went to heaven, you'll find all have snippets of light in them.

I'd like to take you on a journey of stories—of darkness and light, of fear and hope, of worry and peace through the Bible. As you read this book, remember that darkness cannot snuff out light. These Bible stories remind us that **God has given us the light that leads to life.**

Come join me. Let's go on a treasure hunt together, looking for the light of God in the darkest places.

Adam, Eve, and God once walked together, and all was light. But then a sneaky snake convinced the couple to disobey God, and light flickered out. Yet God had a rescue plan: He sent Jesus, the Light that leads to life.

STORY ONE

FROM DARKNESS TO LIGHT

God Made Everything and Loves What He Made

(GENESIS 1–2)

Close your eyes for a second or two. What do you see? Is there any light? Where did the light go?

Now flutter your eyes open. Look around. What do you see?

Did you know that everything you touch, see, feel, smell, and experience was made by God? Every ant, mountain, giant oak tree, blade of grass, and even jumping lemurs—God created them all. And he created me—John, the disciple Jesus loved so much. And guess what? He created you and loves you so much too. I am so excited to share the story of how God made the earth and all the people in it. Lean in—it's a great story!

Before God created this world, everything was like what you see when you close your eyes—darkness. But even in the inky black, God was there, planning his next move. He hovered over the empty world that was covered in deep, dark waters.

DAY ONE

God's voice shook the heavens awake. His words were powerful and clear. He said, "Let there be light." In a flash of brilliance, **light appeared from nowhere, and it chased away the darkness.** God called the light "day," and the darkness he named "night."

This was the earth's first day.

DAY TWO

At first everything was all squished together—you could not tell where the heavens ended and the earth began. So God said, "Let there be a space between the waters, to separate the waters of the heavens from the waters of the earth." When he said this, the earth's blue sky appeared above.

This was the earth's second day.

DAY THREE

Everything was wet and soggy. God said, “Let the waters beneath the sky flow together into one place, so dry ground may appear.” And it did! He called the dry ground “land” and named the waters “seas.”

God noticed that the land and seas were good, and he was joyful.

In an instant, God planted a special garden on the new land. God made sure that every plant dropped its seeds to the ground to form a new baby plant. Every tree would let go of its fruit, and a sapling tree would spring up right beneath it. Sometimes the wind would carry the seeds to other places so that more plants and trees could grow.

God saw that the plants and trees were good.

This was the earth’s third day.

DAY FOUR

Next, God created orbs to hold the light that he had made. He said, "Let these lights in the sky shine down on the earth." He made two lights—a big one to shine in the day and a smaller one to light our way in the night. The day's light was called the sun. The night's light was called the moon.

God wanted the sun, moon, and stars to be signs to help us recognize the days, years, and seasons. That's how winter, spring, summer, and fall all began.

God saw that the sun and moon were good.

This was the earth's fourth day.

At last, it was time for God to make creatures.

He noticed the seas were empty, so he said, "Let the waters swarm with fish and other life." His words came true. Every kind of water animal you can think of, from tiny minnows to great white sharks, from salamanders to bullfrogs, from starfish to dolphins—he created them. They swam and frolicked in the blue waves.

God looked at the sky and crafted every kind of bird you've ever seen (and even more!). From starlings to eagles, robins to hawks, chickadees to albatrosses, they flew and sang in the light of the sun.

God saw that the fish and birds were good.

He blessed the sea creatures and the birds of the sky. He said, "Be fruitful and multiply. Let the fish fill the seas, and let the birds multiply on the earth." When the time was perfect, God blessed all the creatures with babies of their own kind. From east to west, north to south, the world filled with the happy songs of birds.

This was the earth's fifth day.

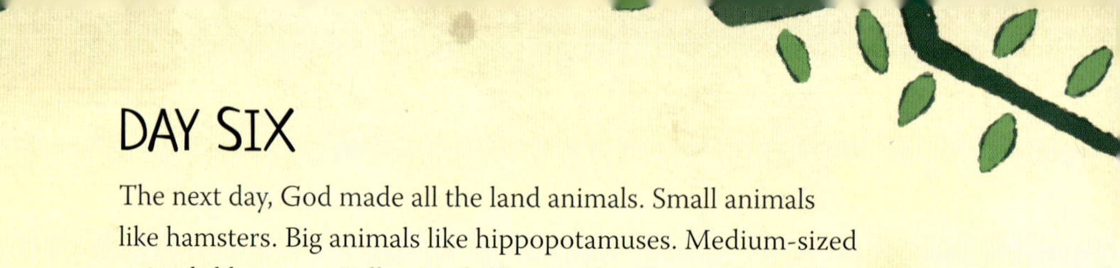

DAY SIX

The next day, God made all the land animals. Small animals like hamsters. Big animals like hippopotamuses. Medium-sized animals like tigers. Tall animals like giraffes. Short animals like minks. Loud animals like hyenas. Quiet animals like rabbits. Furry animals, scaly animals, soft animals, creeping animals—yes, he created these too. He even made dogs and cats and farm animals.

God saw that the animals were good.

And then the God of light did something amazing. He gathered dust from the earth (there had been no rain, so the ground was bone-dry). From the earth's soil, he fashioned a man after his own likeness. He bent low, then breathed air into the man's nose, and the man woke up! He was alive! Imagine what it would feel like to suddenly wake up as a grown person, then see all the animals and birds around you in the middle of a beautiful garden.

The man's name was Adam.

God named this special place he created the garden of Eden. He instructed the man to be Eden's gardener. He was to tend to the ground to help the flowers, plants, and trees grow strong. God pointed to all the trees surrounding Adam, especially two.

A WARNING

One tree was called the tree of life. God gave no instructions about that tree.

But the other special tree was off-limits. God told Adam he could eat fruit from any of the trees except that one. It was called the tree of the knowledge of good and evil. God warned Adam, “If you eat its fruit, you are sure to die.”

Adam stood in the middle of Eden and heard the rush of water all around him. Four rivers brought much-needed water to the garden—the Pishon, the Gihon, the Tigris, and the Euphrates. Everywhere Adam looked, he spied beauty, but God knew it wasn't good for Adam to be alone.

A JOB

So God brought Adam companions—wild animals, farm animals, and birds—and he told the man to name them. Adam named the lynx, the dodo bird, the platypus, and the anteater, and he noticed that each creature had a companion. But there was no companion for Adam, no one to help him tend the garden of Eden in the middle of the four powerful, splashing rivers.

A FRIEND!

So God helped the man to fall asleep, and he performed a special surgery. He removed one of Adam's ribs from his side, then stitched his skin back together.

In a flash, God fashioned a woman from Adam's missing rib. She was also made in the image of God, and God loved her so much. With joy, he presented her to Adam.

Adam was so happy to no longer be alone that he composed a poem about her, and he called her "woman." The two of them did not wear any clothes, which would seem scary to us, but the couple did not think anything of it. They were completely peaceful about their situation in the garden of Eden—in the midst of the four rivers, two special trees, and animals and birds aplenty. And neither of them was lonely.

God noticed this about the woman and the man: They were *very* good.

This was the earth's sixth day.

God created everything we see in six amazing days. The heavens. The earth. The sky. The light. The land. The seas. The sun. The moon. The stars. The fish and birds. The animals. Two people. God made everything he decided to make. **It was no longer dark all the time, and the sun shone every morning.**

DAY SEVEN

On the seventh day, God rested from all that work. He said the seventh day was special because it was the day God rested from making everything. We call this day the Sabbath.

This was Earth's seventh day.

John Reflects

When I look at the stars at night or the mountains behind me or the creatures that creep along the ground, I can't help but thank God for them. Every breath I breathe is a gift from God. The sun shining its light on my face? Gift. The friendship I have with the other disciples? Gift. Isn't it amazing that God created every single thing and person we see?

THE LIGHT MOMENT

God's voice shook the heavens awake, and light chased away the darkness. God put two lights in the sky: the sun and the moon. Then the God of light made animals and humans. And it was no longer dark all the time.

Questions for Conversation

Why do you think God decided to create light at the very beginning of the creation story?

How does light make your life better?

Prayer

Jesus, thank you for making this big, wide world we live in and creating light so we can see all your gifts clearly. Help me be grateful for everything I see today. Amen.

STORY TWO

THE SNEAKY SNAKE

God's Ways Are Best, but We Choose to Sin

(GENESIS 3)

Sometimes, I have a hard time obeying the rules. I've yelled at my brother, I've hit my friends, and I've told my mom a lie. What about you—are you good at obeying? I bet you might be a little bit like me. We all mess up sometimes, and the darkness starts to creep back in again. Well, guess what! There's a reason we disobey. We humans have been messing up for a long time. And it all started back in the very good garden that God created.

ONE RULE

Remember Adam and Eve? They had so much fun in the garden. They played with all the animals and made sure they had everything they needed. All the trees had big, beautiful fruit that Adam and Eve could munch on whenever their tummies grumbled. **And God walked with them every day, and his face shone on them.**

As you might remember from the first story in this book, God only gave them one rule: They couldn't eat of the tree of the knowledge of good and evil. And for a while, they didn't even go near it. **They didn't want to because their home with God sparkled with light and joy.** The birds chirped. The sun shone bright. Nothing died, and nobody got hurt. Everything in the garden God had made was perfect. Adam and Eve loved being with God in his garden.

But one day, everything changed.

THE SNEAKY SNAKE SNEAKS

A sneaky snake slithered his way up to Eve, and he had a question for her. "Did God really say you must not eat the fruit from any of the trees in the garden?"

Now, if you heard a talking snake, what would you do? I would run away—snakes scare me! Maybe you would run, too, or try to trap it in a box or run and tell someone to help. But Eve did something different. She talked back.

"We can eat fruit from all the trees in the garden," she said as she picked a purple fig from a nearby tree. "See?" She took a big, juicy bite and grinned. Out of the corner of her eye, she saw the forbidden tree as she swallowed her bite. "Oh, well . . . God did say there's one tree we can't eat from. That one." She pointed her sticky finger at the tree. "He said if we touch it, we will die."

Then the sneaky snake spoke words of darkness to Eve. "God's just being silly," he hissed. "He knows if you eat that special fruit, you'll become just like him. You'll know all the things he knows—and he knows everything."

Eve thought about what the sneaky snake said. Maybe he was right. Maybe God was keeping a good thing from her and Adam. Maybe if she took just one little bite of the fruit on the forbidden tree, she could know everything. Why would God tell her not to eat from this tree anyway? The fruit looked so good—ripe and yummy and ready to be eaten. Life was very good with God in the garden, but maybe she could make it even better.

She saw the fruit, picked it, and took a big bite.

And then she gave some to Adam, who stood nearby.

EYES OPENED

The moment Eve and Adam swallowed, they opened their eyes and gasped. "Oh no!" they exclaimed. "We don't have any clothes on. We have to hide—God will know we disobeyed."

If you had to make clothes really fast, what would you do? I would grab a fish sack or a shawl. But what could Adam and Eve find? Just some leaves—they were in a garden after all. So they sewed them together as best they could and hid. They had broken God's rule, and they knew what they had done was wrong. They didn't want God's light to shine on them anymore, because they were so embarrassed that he would see what they had done.

What do you think God did? Did he yell in an angry voice? Bang his big fists? Stomp his strong feet?

No. God came looking for them. He said, "Where are you?"

Wait! Do you think God didn't know where they were hiding? He knows everything. He'd known they would mess up, he'd known they would hide, but he'd always had a plan.

Adam and Eve peeked out of their hiding spot, trembling. Adam said, "We were scared because we have no clothes on. So we hid when we heard you coming."

"Who told you that you were naked? Did you eat fruit from the forbidden tree?"

Adam said, "Yeah, but it's her fault." He pointed at Eve. "She gave it to me."

God looked at Eve and said, "What have you done?"

Eve stomped her foot. "Well sure, I gave it to him, but the sneaky snake told me to. It's his fault."

You and I know whose fault it was. Adam and Eve were the ones who disobeyed. They didn't have to listen to the snake, but they did. They ruined the perfect garden and their very good life with God. They now had a very big problem: sin. Sin is anything we do or think or say that breaks God's heart—like disobeying, lying, or stealing. **The darkness of sin had come into the world, and with it, death.**

GOD'S PLAN

But remember, God had a plan. He'd known what Adam and Eve would do, and he knew how to make it right again. He loved his people so much. He couldn't let them get away with disobeying, but he also wanted to rescue them.

God started with the sneaky, sneaky snake. The snake is God's enemy—we call him Satan. God told the snake that someday, one of Eve's great-great-great-great-greaaaaaat-grandkids—a Rescuer—would smoosh his head. The snake would bite this person's heel, but the Rescuer would win in the end.

Then God told Adam and Eve that because they had sinned, they couldn't live in the garden anymore. They could no longer walk with God and feel his light on their faces. Having babies would be hard for Eve, and working the ground would be difficult for Adam. And worst of all, Adam and Eve would die one day. We call these things *consequences*, or the bad things that happen because we sin.

God saw Adam and Eve shaking in their leafy clothes. He made them outfits from animal skins. He loved Adam and Eve so much that he made sure they were warm for their journey outside of the garden.

As they left, God put a big angel to stand guard so Adam and Eve couldn't come back. The angel had a big, flaming sword that shone bright for miles and miles.

John Reflects

This part of the story makes me sad. But don't worry. Remember what God said—a Rescuer was coming. And he would be the Light of the World who would squish the sneaky snake and take away all the bad things that come from sin. He would make it possible for us to walk in God's light again.

THE LIGHT MOMENT

God walked with Adam and Eve in the garden, and their home sparkled with light and joy. But a sneaky snake spoke words of darkness to them, so they disobeyed God—and they hid from God's light. The darkness of sin had come into the world, and with it, death.

Questions for Conversation

When was the last time you disobeyed? Does disobeying feel like being in the sunshine or in the darkness?

What do you think God will do to squish the sneaky snake so we can walk in God's light again?

Prayer

God, I am sorry for the ways I have disobeyed you and hidden from your light. Thank you for having a plan to rescue me from sin. Amen.

STORY THREE

GOD KEEPS HIS PROMISES

Even When People Sin, God Provides a Way Out

(GENESIS 6–9)

Sometimes life is just plain hard, don't you think? When Jesus' other disciples and I were caught in a terrifying storm on the Sea of Galilee, we were so afraid. The sky grew black as night, and I thought everything was lost. So I understand how Adam and Eve must've felt after the sneaky snake convinced them to disobey God and they could no longer stay in Eden with God.

THE FIRST COUPLE

After God put Adam and Eve out of the garden of Eden, the world grew darker and darker because of their choices. The young couple began having kids, who had their own kids, who then had more kids, so the world filled up with people. Yet all these people did not seek out God's friendship. And they kept breaking God's heart with their choices.

God felt sad that he had created people who did such bad things. It seemed like everyone only wanted to hurt others all the time.

ENTER NOAH

But there was one person who shone brightly in the middle of all this darkness.

At 600 years old, Noah was a good man, full of strength, kindness, and faith. He walked closely with God. He had a wife and three sons named Shem, Ham, and Japheth. And those sons had wives too.

People were sinning more and more, and the world seemed darker and scarier than ever. God wanted to rescue Noah and his family from all the chaos. He told Noah to build an ark, a type of large boat. He told him to make it from cypress wood and to coat it in tar all over so it would be waterproof. "Give it three decks and fill it with stalls," God instructed.

Noah must have wondered why God wanted stalls inside. And why so many decks? But before he could ask questions, God told Noah to make the ark 450 feet long, 75 feet wide, and 45 feet high. He instructed him to leave a one-and-a-half-foot-long opening below the roof all the way around the top of the boat and to put a doorway on its side. God told Noah he would bring a mighty flood—and the ark would be a rescue ship for people and animals.

What a strange job God gave Noah, a man who had never built an ark before! He was thankful for such clear instructions from God, but he probably wondered if people would make fun of him for building a giant boat. Even though God's instructions were obvious, Noah had a choice. Would he build a boat in the middle of dry land, or would he not?

THE ARK

Noah obeyed God. He did everything God asked him to do, even if it sounded foolish. That reminds me of the things Jesus asked me to do. Some of them made no sense at the time, but now that I look back on it, I'm so glad I obeyed him. Still, it must've been hard for Noah.

Noah and his sons chopped down mighty cypress trees, then sawed and sanded them into long, smooth planks. Next they built a skeleton for the boat. Then they wrapped the skeleton in bendable wood planks. They made wooden beams and joined them together. They made animal stalls just as God had instructed. And they created living quarters on the upper decks for their family.

People must have come from all the surrounding villages to watch Noah work. Maybe they mocked him and hurled insults.

"What a fool!" someone remarked. "Why are you building a boat in the middle of nowhere?"

"He thinks God spoke to him about such a thing. Want to know what I think? Noah is crazy," another said.

"What a waste of trees," a bystander said, shaking his head.

Still, Noah and his sons continued sawing, pounding, sanding, and joining until their beards were full of sawdust.

At last, Noah waterproofed the ark inside and out with sticky, smelly tar. He worked until his fingers grew weary, his back bent over, and his feet ached. The boat stood tall, firm on the dry earth.

THE MIGHTY FLOOD

The time came when the mighty flood would soon soak the earth, burying it in dark water.

God told Noah and his family to get into the ark and welcome animals, two by two, male and female—including birds and scurrying creatures. The animals came: Wild animals like hyenas. Tame animals like sheep. Large animals like rhinoceroses. Small animals like mice. Every creature you can think of, a girl and boy of each, marched into the ark's open mouth.

Do you think any villagers standing by would help by closing the door to the giant ark? I doubt it. They probably laughed and teased Noah and his family instead.

So it was God who shut the door of the boat from the outside, sealing them securely inside. He told them it would take seven days for the rains to fall.

Noah waited. He looked out the tiny window on the top deck, but only sunshine winked at him. How could a storm come from such a blue sky?

No water spit from the sky. No clouds polka-dotted the blue. No wind, no distant thunder, no hint of a storm. Nothing on day one or two or three or four or five or six—just as God had said. Outside, people shouted at them, mocking Noah's family for doing such a foolish thing.

But Noah knew he had heard the voice of God, even when the sun shone. He had spent over 600 years walking with God, and he knew he could trust the God who created light out of darkness, people from dust, and animals just by speaking.

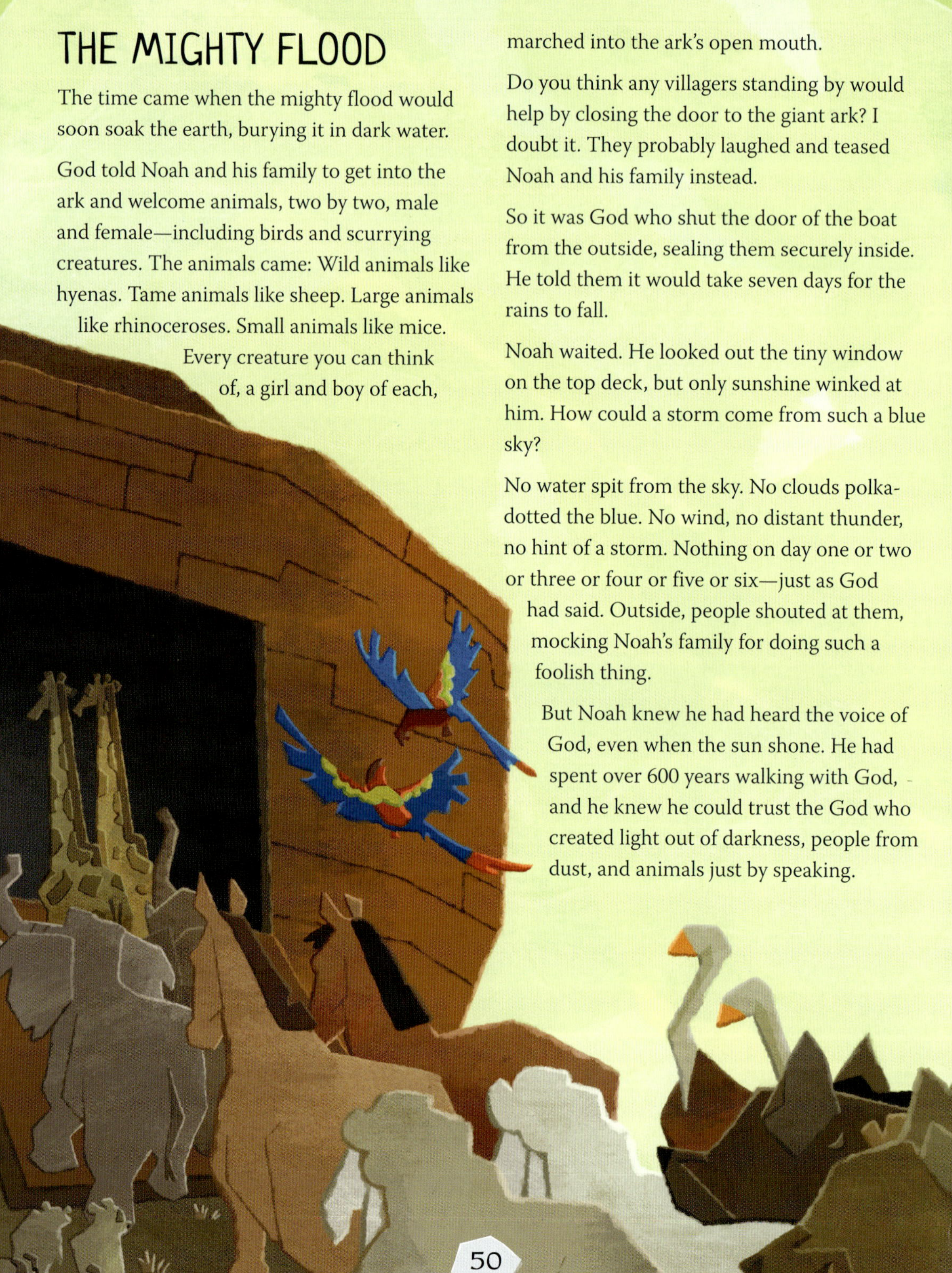

So he waited.

One more day.

A raindrop plinked onto Noah's nose when he looked skyward that morning. The sky, once blue, grew dark as night. When Noah looked downward, gushes of water spewed from the ground like a waterfall falling upward. A torrent of rain pelted the boat. Lightning flashed. Thunder roared back. The dark waters swirled, and the earth rumbled beneath; the ark creaked, rose, then floated safely above the earth's surface. The mighty storm and the spewing fountains lasted day after day after day. Noah and his family were grateful God had instructed them to bring a supply of food, but sometimes the boat rocked so violently that they must have gotten seasick!

A LONG WAIT

They waited.

Forty days. Forty nights.

While the sky remained inky dark.

And the boat sailed past the mountaintops.

Five months went by.

Food got scarce. The animals grew restless. The ark continued to creak and moan.

God remembered Noah, his family, and all the animals. On day 150, God sent a gentle wind to blow across the world. Bit by bit, the floodwaters lessened. The mighty fountains of the deep finally closed their mouths and stopped spurting water. Noah's family had floated for days upon days, but on this day, the boat stopped rocking. Below them, Noah saw that the ark had lodged on the mountains of Ararat.

Still, they waited, stranded on a mountain. Two and a half months went by, and other mountains appeared all around them as the waters sank lower and lower.

Then they waited forty more days.

LETTING BIRDS FLY

Noah decided to let a raven fly from the top window of the ark. The bird flew around but could find no rest.

Then he released a dove. But the dove flew around and could find no place to land. Noah reached his hand from the window, and the dove returned to him.

He waited another seven days. Noah let the dove fly from the ark again, but this time was different. The dove returned. In its beak was a fresh olive leaf. This was encouraging because it meant the flood had completely died down.

Still, Noah waited another week. He released the dove—but this time the bird did not return at all. It had found a nesting place.

All in all, Noah's family stayed in the ark a little over a year before God told them to leave the ark. He then instructed them to let all the animals roam the earth so they could fill it back up with babies.

THE RAINBOW

Noah obeyed God. He built an altar to him out of respect and thanks. God promised Noah that he would never curse the ground again. This promise he made is called a covenant. **Then God told Noah that he would send a shining rainbow as a sign of his promise.**

Noah looked toward the bluest sky. A cloud formed in the west, then briefly darkened the earth. Sheets of rain fell, but the light broke through, and a colorful rainbow followed. Noah knew darkness would never win. The rainbow reminded Noah (and reminds us) that God keeps his promises.

John Reflects

God brought Noah's family safely through the waters, and he promises to be with you through any storm you experience too. God loves to keep his promises.

The flood reminds me of that scary storm I mentioned at the beginning of this story.

When that giant storm blew in on the Sea of Galilee, we thought we would drown. But Jesus stood up and told the waters to be calm, and everything stopped in a quick heartbeat. Jesus showed us that he had power over the wind and sea. And he can calm the storms in your life too.

THE LIGHT MOMENT

After God put Adam and Eve out of the garden, the world grew darker and darker. But one man, Noah, shone in the middle of the darkness. He obeyed God when no one else would—so God lifted him above the dark waters in an ark, and God sent his shining rainbow as a sign of his promise.

Questions for Conversation

What was the scariest storm you've ever experienced? Did it get dark and windy? How did God help you through that storm?

Have you ever seen a rainbow? How about a double rainbow? What did the rainbow look like?

Prayer

Jesus, I'm grateful that you can rescue people from storms, no matter how dark it gets. Thank you for your promises. Next time I see a rainbow, help me remember how kind you are. Amen.

STORY FOUR

STARS IN THE SKY

Faith Makes You Move

(GENESIS 12–21)

What would you do if you had a plan to save the world? Would you get a team together? Maybe some friends or your siblings? Or maybe you could ask your parents or teachers for help? I would see if my brother James could lend a hand. He always knows what to do.

I bet, though, that my plan and even yours might not work out like we'd want it to.

But guess what? God makes plans all the time, and his plans always go how he wants them to go. **How do you think God was going to save the world and shine his light in the dark?**

GOD'S PLAN BEGINS

God had a plan, after all. Back in the garden of Eden, God gave Adam and Eve a little hint about it. Do you remember? God said that one day, one of Eve's great-great-great-great-greaaaaaat-grandkids would smoosh the sneaky snake's head. God planned to work through one big family to bring the Rescuer for all of us.

And that family began with a man named Abraham.

Well, he started off named Abram, but God changed his name to Abraham because he made Abraham an important promise. He told Abraham to go far away from his home to a brand-new land. God promised to keep Abraham safe as he traveled. Best of all, God said he would give Abraham a giant family that would be a blessing to the entire world. That's what Abraham means—father of many.

MORE THAN THE STARS

God took Abraham outside one night. Up above, thousands of stars twinkled, and the moon shone bright. **God said to Abraham, "Look up into the sky and count the stars if you can. That's how many descendants you will have!"**

Do you think you could count all the stars? How many do you think there are? Millions? Billions? There are so many that only God knows the amount. That's a lot of kids and grandkids God promised. A *very* giant family.

Now, there's something else you need to know about Abraham. He was really old—with a long gray beard and wrinkles. His wife, Sarah, was old—way too old to have kids. And worse, they didn't have any children—not a single one.

They were a teeny tiny family, not a giant one. So how was God going to make them a big family that would help the entire world? It seemed impossible.

FAITH MAKES YOU MOVE

Abraham and Sarah didn't know how God would do it, but they had faith. Faith means believing in something even if you can't see it. Abraham and Sarah couldn't see God with their eyes, but they heard what he said and believed in their hearts that he told the truth. And you know what else is amazing about faith? Faith doesn't just happen in your heart. Faith is so powerful that it bursts out of you!

It's like when you feel really silly, and you just have to wiggle around or do a crazy dance. Has that ever happened to you? Faith in God is like that—it makes you move.

So what did Abraham and Sarah do with their wiggly, excited faith? They moved. They followed God wherever he led them. It was like a big adventure! They climbed up, up, up, the mountains and down, down, down the hills. They waded across rivers and rested under tall trees. Sometimes they met rulers and important people. Other times, they found enemies. But God kept his promise. He made sure Abraham and Sarah were safe no matter what happened. And he showed them the path to follow, even when the way seemed dark.

GOD KEEPS HIS PROMISE

This promise God made wasn't any old promise—it was an important promise, a covenant. Just like the one God made with Noah. When God makes a covenant, he will never, ever break it. A covenant that God makes is a promise forever.

But sometimes, God takes a long time to fulfill his promises. Or at least to us, it feels like a long time. That's how Abraham and Sarah felt. They followed God on their big adventure for a long time—over twenty years. Since so much time had passed, they wondered if God would ever give them their giant family. By now, Abraham's beard had grown longer, and Sarah's wrinkles creased her face even more.

One day, three men visited Abraham and Sarah. Abraham spotted them and invited the men over for dinner. Sarah quickly whipped up a yummy meal, and Abraham brought it to them. When their stomachs were full, they asked, "Where is Sarah, your wife?"

"She's inside the tent," Abraham replied.

Then one of them said, "Around this time next year, you and your wife, Sarah, will have a son!"

Sarah could hear them from her spot in the tent, and she laughed. "Those silly men. I am way too old to have a baby now. So is Abraham. I know God promised a child, but that seems impossible."

What Sarah didn't know was that God had sent the three men as his messengers—angels. The passage suggests that one of them was God himself, visiting Abraham. Either way, God heard what Sarah said. So God asked Abraham, "Why did Sarah laugh? Is anything too hard for the Lord?"

What do you think? Is anything too hard for God to do?

You're right. Nothing is too difficult for God! He can do anything. **Even though it seemed impossible to Abraham and Sarah, God kept his forever promise.** One year later, Abraham and Sarah had a baby boy named Isaac.

Their teeny tiny family became a little less teeny. But it still wasn't the giant family God had promised, was it? Not yet at least. God takes his time to fulfill his promises sometimes, but it's okay because he has a plan.

Abraham and Sarah and Isaac were a part of the very start of God's plan, so they only saw the beginning. We're lucky because we get to see how God made their teeny tiny family into a giant one. Jesus—the Light of the World, the Snake Smoosher, and the Rescuer—came from Abraham and Sarah's family tree. Everyone who believes in Jesus gets to be a part of God's family—the family that goes all the way back to Abraham and Sarah—and it's as big as the number of stars in the sky.

John Reflects

When our path seems too dark—when we don't know what God's doing or when something seems impossible, we can be like Abraham and Sarah and have faith in God. When I first put my faith in God, I was so excited that I left everything behind and followed after Jesus—but I'll tell you that story a little later. The point is that faith makes us move—that was true for Abraham and Sarah, it was true for me, and it's also true for you.

THE LIGHT MOMENT

God had a plan to shine light in the dark through one special family. It all began with a man named Abraham. God told Abraham to count the stars because that's how many descendants he would have. Even though it seemed impossible, God kept that promise.

Questions for Conversation

How do you think God planned to bring light to the world through Abraham's family?

When has faith made you move?
What does it look like to show your faith through your actions?

Prayer

God, you are good at keeping your promises. Thank you for always doing what you say you will do. I pray to have faith like Abraham and Sarah, even when the way seems dark. Amen.

STORY FIVE

THE STAIRWAY THAT TOUCHED HEAVEN

God Is Involved in What's Happening on Earth

(GENESIS 25–33, PARTICULARLY 28:10-22)

Do you remember Abraham and his great faith? He sure went through a lot of worry with no child for so many years. God promised him children and land, but those promises often seemed far, far away. Abraham learned to trust God for impossible things, but his journey wasn't easy. Come to think of it, no one's path is ever stick-straight. Mine certainly hasn't been.

I thought Jesus would be creating a strong, new kingdom—and that we would finally be free of the Romans and their rule. But that's not what happened. I didn't realize at the time, but God had something much, much better in mind. I had to wait to find out what that would be, and sometimes God asks all of us to have the same kind of patience, even when we're waiting in the dark.

ABRAHAM'S SON

After Isaac was born, Abraham and Sarah kept getting older and older until the day Sarah died. While Isaac was mourning his mom, God provided Rebekah as a wife for him. **But she was unable to have children, just like Sarah had been.**

Isaac felt sad for Rebekah and worried for himself. How would they survive without kids? You see, in those days, there were no safety nets for people who grew old. The only way to be taken care of was to have children who loved you and made sure you were doing well. **Their future looked dark.**

Isaac cried out to God, "God, please bring us children!" He looked to the sky, much like his father Abraham had done.

AN ANSWERED PRAYER

In time, God answered his prayer twofold! Rebekah would have twin boys. Even when she carried them within her, they wrestled with each other.

They kicked and kicked. "Why is this happening to me?" she asked God one day.

God answered, "The sons in your womb will become two nations. From the very beginning, the two nations will be rivals. One nation will be stronger than the other; and your older son will serve your younger son." This was not the way things typically happened. Usually the eldest would be the boss of the youngest.

When Rebekah gave birth, Esau came out first, followed by Jacob, who was grabbing Esau's heel. That's why they named him Jacob—his name means "heel holder."

TWINS

Like they had done before they were born, the brothers often fought. Jacob grew to be a trickster, and he deceived his father, Isaac, and took his brother Esau's blessing. He wanted to harm his brother—he was acting just like that sneaky snake, telling lies and walking in darkness. As a result, Esau hated Jacob and plotted to kill him.

Rebekah heard of Esau's plan, so she pulled Jacob aside. She encouraged him to flee to her brother Laban who lived in Haran. She said, "Stay there with him until your brother cools off. When he calms down and forgets what you have done to him, I will send for you to come back."

JACOB RUNS AWAY

Fearful and looking behind him all the way, Jacob fled from his home in Beersheba toward Haran. He didn't stop until the sun sank into the night sky near a town called Luz. He let out a long breath, worried about Esau's plans and feeling lonely. He set up a tent, built a crackling fire, and ate. All that running had tired him out, so he found a stone to use as a pillow.

But this was no ordinary night.

A DREAM

When Jacob closed his eyes in the darkness of night, he had a dream. It felt so real, so vivid. In it, a giant stairway reached all the way to heaven, its bottom step on the earth. Brilliant angelic beings went up and down the stairway.

For a moment, Jacob was too overwhelmed to look beyond the giant stairway. Just seeing the angels moving between heaven and earth frightened him. But eventually he looked all the way to the top of the stairway, heart pounding.

At the stairway's top stood the Lord!

How could this be possible? Jacob knew that no one could see the Lord and live. He trembled as light shone all around.

A CONVERSATION

God spoke. "I am the Lord, the God of your grandfather Abraham, and the God of your father, Isaac."

Jacob fell to the dusty earth, tasting dirt.

God said, "The ground you are lying on belongs to you. I am giving it to you and your descendants."

Jacob must have thought, *I don't have a wife! I certainly don't have children yet.*

But God continued from the glowing heavens. "Your descendants will be as numerous as the dust of the earth! They will spread out in all directions—to the west and the east, to the north and the south."

Jacob, terrified, lifted his head, daring to look north, south, east, and west. Could these words come true? Who was he that God would speak such kindness?

God thundered, "And all the families of the earth will be blessed through you and your descendants."

Jacob knew God had promised the same blessings to his grandfather Abraham. Suddenly he felt very small, quite unworthy of all these amazing words.

God continued, "What's more, I am with you, and I will protect you wherever you go. One day I will bring you back to this land. I will not leave you until I have finished giving you everything I have promised you."

A MEMORIAL

With a start, Jacob woke up in the middle of the night, lifted his head from his rock pillow and let out a long-held breath. Even though he was alone, he spoke to himself, his voice quivering in fear. "Surely the Lord is in this place, and I wasn't even aware of it!" He remembered fearing his brother Esau and how he'd spent the day huffing and puffing as he ran away from him. He looked toward the heavens while little starry lights poked the sky. "What an awesome place this is!" he said. "It is none other than the house of God, the very gateway to heaven!"

The next morning, Jacob rose with the sun. He grabbed the stone pillow and set it upright like a pillar. He took a flask from his provisions, then poured olive oil over the rock. "I am naming this place Bethel," he said. Bethel means "house of God." He touched the pillar. He said the stone would be a place where everyone could remember what God had done, where they could worship him.

WHAT HAPPENED NEXT

Jacob eventually reached his destination. There he worked for his Uncle Laban, married two wives, and had many sons. But Laban treated Jacob and his family poorly, so they fled (once again!) toward Bethel, the place where the stairway had been. On this journey, Jacob knew he was going to see Esau again, and he was scared.

A WRESTLING MATCH

That night Jacob, who had wrestled with Esau in the womb, had a wrestling match with God! God touched Jacob's hip, taking it out of the socket, yet still Jacob wrestled. He would not let go of God until God blessed him yet again.

"What is your name?" God asked.

"Jacob."

God said, "Your name will no longer be Jacob. From now on you will be called Israel, because you have fought with God and with men and have won." God had renamed Jacob, the "heel holder," and called him Israel, which means "to wrestle with God." From that point on, the one who had wrestled with God walked with a limp.

And guess what? When he finally met Esau again, instead of hurting Jacob, Esau gave his brother a big hug. What a surprise!

John Reflects

Did you know that Israel used to be named Jacob? It took a long time for Jacob to become Israel, and I'm sure he grew tired from all that walking. Often when we (Jesus' disciples) were following in Jesus' footsteps, we, too, would grow tired. We had no tent, so we slept under the stars, using rocks as pillows just as Jacob did. We learned that God was kind to us even when we didn't know where we would sleep or what we would eat. In the hard times, we learned to trust Jesus. That's my hope for you too.

THE LIGHT MOMENT

Isaac and his wife, Rebekah, couldn't have children, and their future looked dark. But God answered Isaac's prayer, and Rebekah had twin boys. The younger son, Jacob, stole his brother's blessing, living in the dark. But God had plans to keep his promise to Abraham through Jacob.

Questions for Conversation

Was Jacob walking in the dark or the light when he lied and stole from his brother? What about when he wrestled with God and asked God to bless him?

What did you learn about God in this story? How did God treat Jacob? What did Jacob do as a result?

Prayer

Jesus, sometimes I feel like I'm wandering around, not finding my way. Please light my path and show me the next step. Help me to love others who are hard to get along with too. Amen.

FROM PIT TO PRISONER TO PROTECTOR

God Is Always Up to Something, Even When It Doesn't Seem Like It

(GENESIS 37–50)

I love scavenger hunts. Have you ever done one? My brother James and I would do them all the time when we were little. He'd hide little things like fishhooks and beads all around our home, and I'd have to find them. I liked searching high and low for all the treasures hidden in unlikely places. It's fun feeling like you're on an adventure, and it's exciting to find what you've been looking for.

Scavenger hunts remind me of Joseph's story. His life was wild—full of so many ups and downs. On the surface, it might look like God wasn't helping Joseph at all. But if we see his life as a scavenger hunt, we can find all the ways God worked in secret, special ways to help Joseph and his whole family.

JEALOUS BROTHERS

In our last story, we met Jacob, who was also called Israel. **Jacob had twelve sons, and one of them was named Joseph. Jacob loved Joseph very much**—so much that he gave him a coat filled with color and beauty. Joseph loved wearing his colorful coat. But his brothers were jealous. They wanted the coat and to be recognized by their dad just like Joseph had been.

Soon after, Joseph had two dreams. In both, he dreamt that his brothers all bowed down to him. When he told his brothers about the dreams, they raged with anger. They wouldn't bow down to their little brother—no way! Their jealousy boiled up so much that one day, they decided to get back at him.

THE PIT

The brothers made a plan. They wanted to kill Joseph, but Reuben, the oldest, said they should capture him and throw him in a large pit instead. Reuben decided that he would secretly rescue Joseph later.

The brothers' plan worked like a charm, and Joseph fell all the way down into the dark hole. It was empty and lonely down there. How do you think Joseph felt? He must have been scared and confused. Why would his brothers be so mean?

Before Reuben could rescue Joseph, the brothers came up with an even meaner plan. They saw some slave traders coming down the road. They said to each other, "Instead of hurting him, let's sell him." And so they did.

SOLD INTO SLAVERY

The slave traders dragged Joseph off to Egypt, and the brothers returned home. They lied to their father Jacob and said Joseph was killed by a wild animal. Jacob cried and cried. He missed his son and thought he would never see him again.

Joseph made it all the way to the far, far away land of Egypt. An important man named Potiphar became his master, and Joseph helped him take care of his home. Joseph was very good at his job. He scrubbed the floors until they sparkled and cleaned up all the messes—and God blessed everything he did.

Why do you think Joseph could be at peace while doing all these chores? **He knew God was with him, even though he was in a difficult situation.** In the same way, God never leaves us behind. He's always up to something, even if we can't see him. Joseph held tight to that truth as he worked hard for Potiphar. It was like his own version of a scavenger hunt. He looked for God and trusted he was there.

God helped Joseph do all his work so well that Potiphar noticed. He promoted Joseph to the most important job in the whole house! He was in charge of everything. But then Potiphar's wife became angry at Joseph, just like his brothers were. Her anger raged, and she told her husband a lie about Joseph. Potiphar believed the lie and threw Joseph into prison.

PRISONER

Even though Joseph was a slave, he'd had some power in Potiphar's house. But now he was in prison! Darkness surrounded Joseph in that cold, dark place. He was alone again. He could have given up. But instead, he kept trusting that God was with him. He worked really hard, and God helped him again. Before long, Joseph was in charge of everyone in the prison.

Two workers from the king's house—a baker and a cupbearer—were thrown into prison. They had confusing dreams, and they didn't know what they meant. They asked Joseph, and God told Joseph what the dreams meant: The baker would be punished, but the cupbearer would be set free. Joseph asked the cupbearer if he would tell the king (called Pharaoh) about Joseph's situation, and the man promised he would.

Everything Joseph said came true! But instead of asking Pharaoh to free Joseph, the cupbearer forgot all about him. Do you think Joseph was sad? He waited and waited and waited, but he stayed locked in that prison.

PROTECTOR

Then, just when it seemed Joseph would never be free, a ray of light broke through. Pharaoh had scary dreams. He needed someone to tell him what they meant. The cupbearer remembered Joseph and told Pharaoh, "Go ask Joseph! He knows how to interpret dreams."

So Pharaoh summoned Joseph to his palace. Pharaoh explained his scary dreams—he had seen healthy cows and sick cows, healthy wheat and sick wheat. God helped Joseph understand the confusing dreams, and Joseph told the king what God said: After seven years of lots of harvest, there was going to be a famine—that means there would be no food anywhere and everyone would be very hungry. Pharaoh needed to store up food so the kingdom would be protected when all the food went away.

Pharaoh marveled at Joseph's words. He was so impressed that he made Joseph the second-in-command of the entire kingdom to help them prepare for the famine. **God brought Joseph all the way from the pit to the prison to be the protector of all of Egypt.**

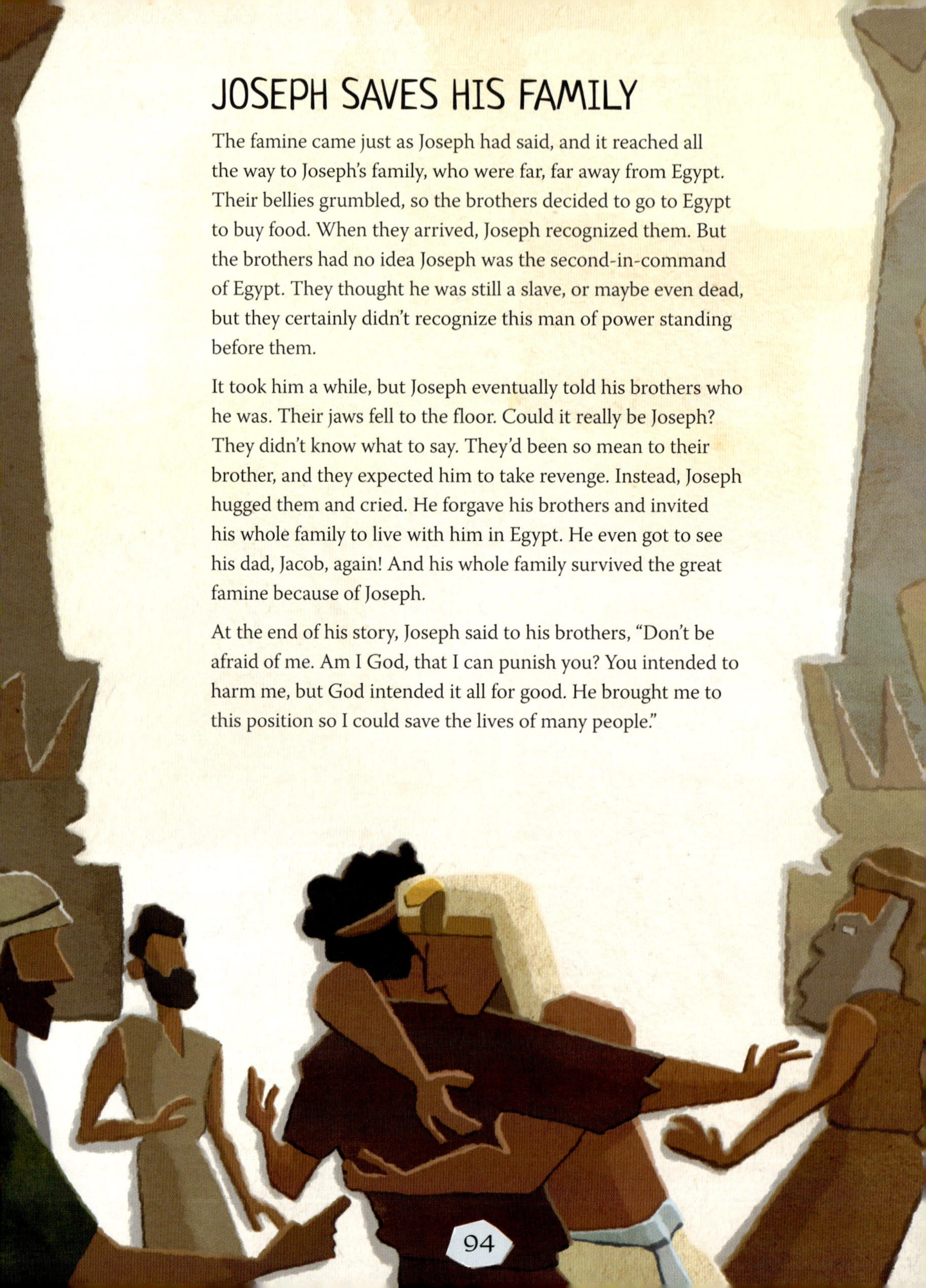

JOSEPH SAVES HIS FAMILY

The famine came just as Joseph had said, and it reached all the way to Joseph's family, who were far, far away from Egypt. Their bellies grumbled, so the brothers decided to go to Egypt to buy food. When they arrived, Joseph recognized them. But the brothers had no idea Joseph was the second-in-command of Egypt. They thought he was still a slave, or maybe even dead, but they certainly didn't recognize this man of power standing before them.

It took him a while, but Joseph eventually told his brothers who he was. Their jaws fell to the floor. Could it really be Joseph? They didn't know what to say. They'd been so mean to their brother, and they expected him to take revenge. Instead, Joseph hugged them and cried. He forgave his brothers and invited his whole family to live with him in Egypt. He even got to see his dad, Jacob, again! And his whole family survived the great famine because of Joseph.

At the end of his story, Joseph said to his brothers, "Don't be afraid of me. Am I God, that I can punish you? You intended to harm me, but God intended it all for good. He brought me to this position so I could save the lives of many people."

CAN YOU FIND GOD'S LIGHT?

Joseph viewed his life as a scavenger hunt. He looked for God even when his life seemed full of darkness. In the pitch black of the pit and the prison, he saw God's light shining. When he was placed in charge of Egypt, he knew God had a purpose for putting him there because God's always up to something good, even when we can't see him.

John Reflects

I think you and I should see our lives as scavenger hunts too. Sometimes we may feel like we're surrounded by darkness. But God's always there—we can trust him just like Joseph did. Let's look for God's light everywhere. He's always up to something good. We just have to look for him.

THE LIGHT MOMENT

Joseph's brothers threw him in a deep, dark pit. He went to a far country and a dirty prison—but God was with him, even there. Just when it seemed Joseph would never be free, a ray of light broke through. God brought Joseph all the way from the pit to the prison to the palace to rescue his family—and all of Egypt.

Questions for Conversation

How do you feel when you're in the dark? What helps you not be afraid? What do you think helped Joseph not be afraid when he was in dark places?

What's one way you see God doing something good in your life? Take a moment to thank God for that good thing.

Prayer

God, you are always with me, even when I can't see. Thank you for all your good gifts. Thank you for shining light in the darkness. Amen.

STORY SEVEN

THE FLAMING BUSH

God Hears When His People Cry Out to Him

(EXODUS 1–4)

I never saw a flaming bush—but let me tell you about the time Peter, James, Jesus, and I spent time on a mountain. In an instant, Jesus transformed before our eyes (we were so afraid). He was radiant—brighter than the sun! And he spoke with Moses, who you'll meet today, and Elijah, who you'll meet in story fifteen. A bright cloud overshadowed everything, and God's voice thundered, "This is my dearly loved Son, who brings me great joy. Listen to him."

We fell to the ground. And when it was all over, the light faded, and the only one standing was Jesus. Long before Jesus was born, Moses had a similar experience with the powerful light of God.

HISTORY OF THE PEOPLE OF GOD

Let's remember what a wonderful thing Joseph did—he saved his brothers and his father during a time when there was hardly any food. Remember what that time was called? Yes, a famine. The people of God, the nation of Israel, enjoyed many years of growth and happiness. They had families. Their children grew up, got married, and then had more children. God blessed Israel so much that they grew to be as numerous as the sand in the desert.

But eventually Pharaoh died, and other pharaohs rose to power. They didn't care about Joseph or his family. The new pharaoh worried that the people of Israel would rise up and fight against the nation of Egypt. So he made the Israelites work and work and work until their hands were raw from working so much. He forced them to make bricks in the heat of the day and to labor and harvest in the sweaty fields.

A TERRIBLE LAW

Pharaoh didn't want the Israelites to have any more baby boys because boys grew up to be men, and men could pick up arrows and swords and fight. So he made a terrible law. He called the women who helped the Israelite, or Hebrew, mothers give birth and told them to kill any baby boys.

But the mothers' helpers worried more about what God thought than what Pharaoh wanted. They protected the baby boys. Pharaoh got so angry with them that he made a new decree for the nation of Egypt. "Throw every newborn Hebrew boy into the Nile River," he declared. What a dark time for the Israelites!

Still, the people of God had more and more children.

BABY MOSES

One day a Hebrew couple had a special baby boy. He was delightful! And oh, how they loved this baby. They hid the tiny baby for three short months. But soon his cries grew stronger. They could no longer keep this secret. The baby's mom gently placed the baby into a tar-covered basket of reeds (just like the tar that held together Noah's ark!) and sent him down the Nile River, hoping he would be okay. Miriam, the boy's sister, watched as the baby floated toward Pharaoh's palace.

Pharaoh's daughter, a princess, had come to the mighty river to bathe. She noticed the basket and asked one of her attendants to retrieve it. She bent toward the little boat, removed the reed covering, and saw a crying baby. "This must be one of the Hebrew children," she said.

That's when Miriam dared to approach the royal princess. "Should I go and find one of the Hebrew women to nurse the baby for you?"

The princess agreed—and Miriam brought back the child's mother! Much to her delight, she had the joy of being able to nourish her baby son.

The day came, though, when his mom had to give the toddler to the Egyptian princess. She adopted the boy and called him Moses, which means "saved from the water." That makes sense, doesn't it?

MOSES GOT MAD

Moses grew up in the royal palace of Egypt. He was grateful to be alive, but he also noticed that the Egyptians did not treat his people very well. This made him quite angry, so he decided to help them. One day Moses saw an Egyptian beating one of the Israelites. He looked to the left and to the right. No one else was around! So Moses killed the Egyptian, then quickly buried him in the sand.

The next day, Moses watched sadly as two Hebrew men got in a fist fight. He cried, “Why are you beating up your friend?”

He expected to be thanked. But one of the fighters spit and said, “Who appointed you to be our prince and judge? Are you going to kill me as you killed that Egyptian yesterday?”

MOSES FLED

Moses's heart hammered wildly. He realized everyone knew he was a murderer—so like Jacob who fled from Esau, he ran all the way to a place called Midian and settled with a family of shepherds and shepherdesses. He started his own family there, but he must have thought often of the land of Egypt where his people were enslaved.

Moses tended sheep. That was his job. He watched over the poor animals, rescuing them after they jumped into ditches, or when their feet got stuck in the mud. He learned so much about how to take care of animals. He didn't realize that God was using this dark time in the wilderness to train him to shepherd his people.

A STRANGE SIGHT

One day Moses led his sheep to a place where very little grass grew, and no person was around for miles and miles. He rested his flock at the base of Mount Sinai, known as the mountain of God. He sat down heavily on a rock, wondering when he would be able to return to his people.

That's when he spied the fire, blazing hot to his left. He stood and walked toward the flames. What he saw made little sense to him. A giant bush with brittle stems, shiny leaves, and little flowers held the flame within it. Moses wondered, "Why isn't that bush burning up?" He walked closer.

"Moses! Moses!" **The voice of God resounded powerfully from the middle of the bush.**

Moses trembled. He looked around. The bush still held the flame, but did not crackle in the fire. "Here I am," Moses said.

"Do not come any closer," God warned.

Moses stopped and pulled in a breath. He tried to steady himself. What could this mean?

"Take off your sandals, for you are standing on holy ground."

Moses obeyed, untying his leather sandals and placing them in the dust. His toes felt heat from the fire. He stepped back.

"I am the God of your father—the God of Abraham, the God of Isaac, and the God of Jacob."

In a flash, Moses covered his face with his robe. He was terrified, afraid to look at God.

GOD SENT MOSES

God told Moses that he heard the cries of his people, that he was aware they suffered and were made into slaves. **He spoke of rescuing them, then leading them to a land flowing with milk from cows and sheep, and honey from all the flowers and plants—a new, beautiful homeland where they could be free.** "The cry of the people of Israel has reached me, and I have seen how harshly the Egyptians abuse them," God said.

Moses could still not look at God. His knees buckled.

"Now go, for I am sending you to Pharaoh. You must lead my people Israel out of Egypt."

Only then did Moses pull his face from his cloak. He shook his head. "Who am I to appear before Pharaoh? Who am I to lead the people of Israel out of Egypt?" His words came out small and pinched.

God told Moses he would surely be with him—he didn't have to be afraid because he would be with him every step of the way. "When you have brought the people out of Egypt, you will worship God at this very mountain."

Moses looked up at the rocky sides of Mount Sinai. How could so many people leave a land ruled by such a powerful leader and come here? It was so far away—and across a desert. Moses felt completely unable to do such a gigantic task. So he stalled. He asked God what his name was in case the Israelites wondered who had given Moses such an impossible job.

GOD IS BIG

"I Am who I Am," God replied. "Say this to the people of Israel: I Am has sent me to you." **The bush still blazed but didn't burn up.** God promised Moses that the elders of the land would eventually accept Moses, and that he would deliver the people of Israel through miracles and wonders and signs. When they left their land of slavery, they would ask the Egyptians for silver and gold and beautiful clothing—and they would take the wealth of Egypt with them.

Still, Moses was frightened. Wouldn't you be? He had been in this wilderness forty long years, tending sheep. His own exile would one day mirror Israel's future wandering in the wilderness.

Moses tried to argue with God. There must be someone else to do this great work.

MIRACLES

"What is that in your hand?" God asked Moses.

"A shepherd's staff," Moses said.

God told him to throw the staff to the ground, so he obeyed. Instead of a staff, a wriggling snake slithered in the dust. Moses hollered and jumped away.

"Reach out and grab its tail," God instructed.

How would you feel? Wouldn't it be scary to grab a snake's tail? But Moses nabbed it, and once again the snake became a shepherd's walking stick. God told him to perform this sign for the Egyptians, but Moses was still afraid. So God told Moses to put his hand inside his cloak.

Moses did. When he pulled out his hand, it was white as chalk—full of a terrible and incurable disease called leprosy. God told him to return the leprous hand back to his cloak, and when he did, his skin became fresh and smooth—completely healed. God also told him that if he poured out the Nile's water on the ground, it would instantly become blood. All these signs were to help Moses be brave.

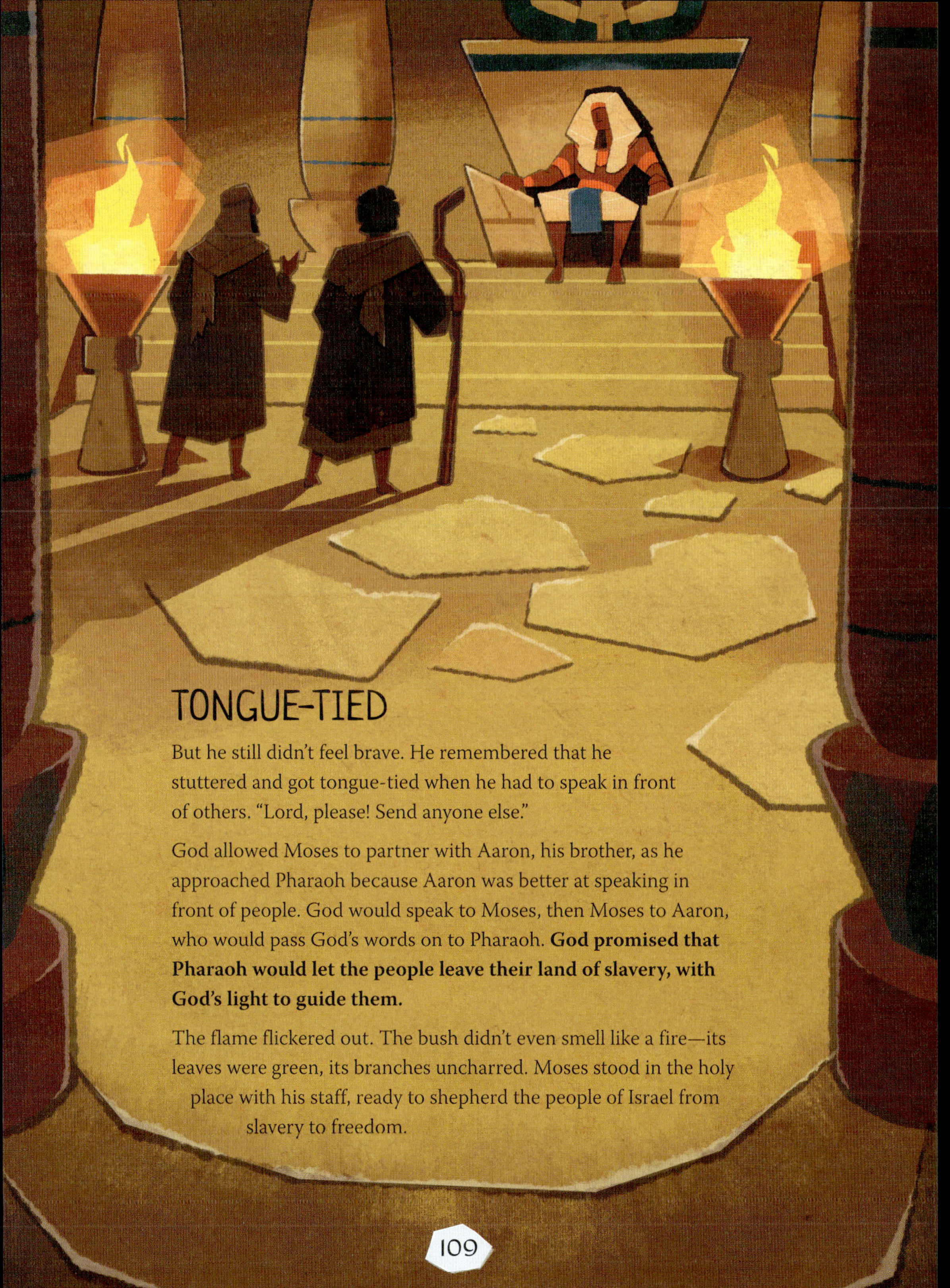

TONGUE-TIED

But he still didn't feel brave. He remembered that he stuttered and got tongue-tied when he had to speak in front of others. "Lord, please! Send anyone else."

God allowed Moses to partner with Aaron, his brother, as he approached Pharaoh because Aaron was better at speaking in front of people. God would speak to Moses, then Moses to Aaron, who would pass God's words on to Pharaoh. **God promised that Pharaoh would let the people leave their land of slavery, with God's light to guide them.**

The flame flickered out. The bush didn't even smell like a fire—its leaves were green, its branches uncharred. Moses stood in the holy place with his staff, ready to shepherd the people of Israel from slavery to freedom.

John Reflects

I remember when my friend Peter cried out to Jesus.

Jesus walked toward us on the water when we were in another storm on the Sea of Galilee. We were all terrified!

But Jesus called Peter to step out of the boat and walk on the water. Can you imagine? For a little moment, Peter actually walked on the water! But then he began to sink into the waves. He asked Jesus to help him—and he did. Just like God listened when his people cried out to him in Egypt, he also listened to Peter. And he hears you too.

THE LIGHT MOMENT

Moses fled Egypt in disgrace, but then God spoke to him from a fiery bush that blazed but didn't burn up. Moses was afraid to go to Pharaoh, yet God promised to help him lead the Israelites out of slavery to a beautiful land—with God's light to guide them.

Questions for Conversation

When was the last time you sat in front of a fire?
What happened to the wood and paper when someone fed it to the fire?
Why do you think the bush Moses saw didn't burn up?

Have you ever felt like your difficult and dark problem was too hard for God? How did God help you through that worry?

Prayer

Jesus, thank you for teaching me about bravery through Moses today—and that even if I am scared, you will light my way through. Amen.

STORY EIGHT

WHEN GOD WAS CLOUD AND FIRE

God Rescues His People and Keeps Them Safe

(EXODUS 5–13)

God is a Rescuer. He hates it when his people are enslaved, so he does everything he can to free them from darkness. I love this part of the story because it reminds me of what Jesus did for you and me. Israel was stuck in slavery in Egypt. We're stuck, too, before we believe in Jesus, except we're in slavery to sin and death. But God had a different plan. Let's see how he freed Israel.

MOSES GOES TO PHARAOH

Moses had been given a mission. God sent him to Egypt to free Israel, and when God calls you to do something, it's best to obey. So even though he was nervous, Moses went. **He and his brother, Aaron, visited Pharaoh and told him, "This is what the Lord, the God of Israel, says: Let my people go!"**

But Pharaoh laughed. "Who is the Lord? Why should I listen to him and let Israel go? I don't know the Lord, and I will not let Israel go."

Uh-oh. Pharaoh refused to let Israel go free. Worse, he commanded the people in charge of the Israelite slaves to make their work tougher and more tiring. What would God do about it? We know God is more powerful than anyone. He could have snapped his fingers, and Israel would have been in the Promised Land in a flash. Their chains would have clattered to the ground with a great crash, and they'd all have jumped up and down for joy. But he didn't do that. Why?

Because God had a better idea. He would free Israel in a way that would show them that he is powerful, he is a Rescuer, and he loves them. He is always ready to shine his light into our darkness.

Pharaoh was going to learn his lesson too. God told Moses, "Now you will see what I will do to Pharaoh. When he feels the force of my strong hand, he will let the people go. In fact, he will force them to leave his land!"

A MIRACLE

Moses and Aaron went back to Pharaoh, and this time, Pharaoh demanded a sign. Aaron threw his wooden staff on the ground. It clattered and hissed—then it turned into a snake! God repeated the same miracle he had done for Moses at the burning bush. But Pharaoh just rolled his eyes. "My magicians can do the same thing. That's not impressive."

His magicians used their tricks to make their staffs into snakes too. But Aaron's snake gobbled up the magician's snakes. Even still, Pharaoh wouldn't budge. He wouldn't let Israel go.

THE FIRST PLAGUE

God wanted to show Pharaoh who was in charge. He directed Moses and Aaron to go down to the Nile River the next morning. They warned Pharaoh that since he wouldn't let Israel go, God would turn their river into blood. All the fish would die, and no one would have water to drink. But Pharaoh crossed his arms and shook his head. So Aaron hit his staff on the water, and it turned blood red.

Pharaoh yawned. "I've seen that before too," he said, and he waved his magicians over. They didn't have God's power, but they used their dark ways to imitate what God had done.

"See?" Pharaoh scoffed. "Your God isn't all that powerful. I can keep Israel here no matter what he says."

THE NEXT EIGHT PLAGUES

Well, God wouldn't be bested by Pharaoh. He sent ten plagues—big and bad problems that affected everyone in Egypt, except the Israelites—to show Pharaoh his power and convince him to let Israel go. The river of blood was first. Then came the frogs—so many hopped up from the river that they covered everyone's houses and stables and even their beds! God sent gnats, and even the magicians couldn't make those pesky bugs appear. After that, flies swarmed in masses all around Egypt. Then the next five plagues happened one after another: The animals became sick, the people and animals got boils (large sores that hurt a lot), hail came down all over the land, locusts (a really destructive and hungry kind of grasshopper) swarmed the crops, and darkness covered Egypt for three days.

After each plague, God sent Moses to tell Pharaoh to let Israel go, and every time, Pharaoh said, "No!" He hardened his heart, which means he said no to God so many times that he refused to listen to God at all. So God kept raining down plagues. But with every plague, God kept Israel safe.

THE TENTH PLAGUE AND THE SPECIAL MEAL

Did you count all the plagues? There's only one left.

The tenth plague. It's the saddest one of all. God told Pharaoh through Moses that if he didn't free Israel, all the firstborn sons of every person and animal in Egypt would die. Did Pharaoh listen? No.

So God sent an angel of death to Egypt, and everything happened just as God had said it would.

But God kept Israel safe. He gave them a special way to show the angel of death they were God's people so that the angel would pass over their homes. They killed a lamb, ate it, and used its blood to mark their doorposts. This meal turned into an annual celebration for Israel to remember that God saved them—it's called Passover because the angel passed over their homes. Get it?

ISRAEL CAN LEAVE

Finally, Pharaoh gave up. He let Israel go. So the Israelites hurried to pack their bags and prepare their animals. They rushed away before Pharaoh could change his mind. But there was a problem: They didn't know the way! They'd never left Egypt before, so they could easily get lost.

God knew what they needed. **His presence swirled above them like a tall cloud during the day, guiding the way. And at night, he showed up as a giant column of flame burning in the sky. He lit their path and kept them safe.**

He led them to a tremendous sea called the Red Sea. The waves crashed so high that the Israelites couldn't wade across. Just as they arrived at the shore, they turned around and saw the Egyptians. Pharaoh had changed his mind! He wanted the Israelites back as slaves, and he raced to capture them again.

GOD RESCUES ISRAEL

Pharaoh should have known better. God can do anything, and he loves his people. He wouldn't let them get trapped and taken back into slavery after he had rescued them. He spoke to Moses, saying, "Pick up your staff and raise your hand over the sea. Divide the water so the Israelites can walk through the middle of the sea on dry ground."

So Moses raised his staff into the air and slammed it down into the sea. The waves rushed up, up, up like two towers, leaving a dry path in between. All the moms and dads and kids and grandparents cheered. God had rescued them again! They all crossed over on the land God cleared for them through the sea.

Pharaoh and his men tried to follow, but God swallowed them up in the water. God's people were safe and free at last.

John Reflects

God loves to save his people. This story is one of my favorites because it shows me how powerful God is and how much he will do to make sure his people are free. We call this the exodus, meaning "the way out," because God made a way for Israel to leave slavery behind in Egypt. God has saved us too. If we believe in Jesus, God frees us from the darkness of sin and death forever. We can experience our own kind of exodus as we walk into his light! All we have to do is believe in Jesus.

THE LIGHT MOMENT

God is a rescuer who does everything he can to free his people from darkness. He sent Moses to tell Pharaoh, "Let my people go!" Pharaoh tried to keep them from leaving—but God was more powerful. As they began their journey, God's presence swirled above them like a cloud and a flame. He lit their path and kept them safe.

Questions for Conversation

Who was more powerful: God or Pharaoh?
What did God do to show how powerful he was?

God freed Israel, and he frees us from the darkness of sin and death when we believe in Jesus. Do you believe Jesus has rescued you?

Prayer

God, you are powerful to rescue us from the darkness. You saved Israel, and you can save me too. I believe in you. Thank you for rescuing me. Amen.

STORY NINE

THE BIG, BRIGHT TEN

God Tells Us What Is Best Because He Loves Us

(EXODUS 19–20)

You may have heard about the Ten Commandments. **God created ten rules to help our world run smoothly** so that people wouldn't hurt each other or God. Jesus spoke of them and often taught about how important it was to be someone who loved God fiercely and was kind to others.

But do you know how the Ten Commandments first came about?

TWO MONTHS

The Ten Commandments all started with a man and a mountain.

That man was Moses, who led the people out of Egypt. You've met him already.

That mountain was Mount Sinai, where Moses first met with God in the flaming bush that never burned up.

Sweaty and tired, with grit in their teeth and dust between their toes, Moses and the Israelites trudged through the desert, worried about water and food. After many days of wandering, they arrived at the base of Mount Sinai. One step at a time, Moses climbed up the mountain to meet with God.

God gave him a special message for the Israelites: "I carried you on eagles' wings," he said. "Obey me and keep my covenant."

Moses remembered how much God had cared for him and the people of Israel. He liked the idea of being carried as if by a soaring eagle.

The last thing God told him was this: "You will be my kingdom of priests, my holy nation."

What a promise! They went from working as slaves for Pharaoh to being God's special nation. Moses hurried down the mountain to tell the people what God had said.

THE PEOPLE LISTEN

All the Israelites replied, "We will do everything the Lord has commanded." Moses climbed back up the mountain and shared this answer with God, who then gave him specific instructions about what would come next. The people were not allowed to come near Mount Sinai while God was meeting with Moses in a cloud, so they marked off a line around the mountain so no one would cross it. But after someone blew a ram's horn, then they could come near.

After three long days, there was terrible thunder and lightning. A gigantic dark cloud crawled from Mount Sinai's top to the bottom near the boundary line because God had come down on the mountain. Someone blew a long, loud blast from a ram's horn to call the people. The wind spun in circles. Everyone shivered as they stood at the mountain's foot. Smoke and fire swirled all around the base of the mountain. Flames and dust flew into the sky.

THE CONVERSATION

The mountain quaked, making the ground shudder.

The ram's horn blew, long and distant.

Moses spoke to the cloud.

God's reply was thunder, thunder, thunder.

God told Moses to remind the people not to climb the mountain, but they were too scared to do it anyway. Then God told Moses that Aaron could hike up Mount Sinai with him.

The thundering voice of God gave these instructions to Moses and Aaron: the Ten Commandments.

THE FIRST FOUR

One. "You must not have any other god but me." There is only one God, and we are invited to love him only.

Two. "You must not make for yourself an idol of any kind or an image of anything in the heavens or on the earth or in the sea." An idol is something you love more than God. It's something that replaces him with something smaller. An idol is something you make, like a statue.

Three. "You must not misuse the name of the Lord your God." God's name is special. We must be careful when we mention it not to spoil it or make it seem small.

Four. "Remember to observe the Sabbath day by keeping it holy." Remember when God made the world in six days, then rested on the seventh? That's what this commandment is about. To rest one day a week means we trust God to provide for us. Resting reminds us that God is God and we are not.

Do you notice something about the first four commandments? What relationship are they talking about?

These four are about our relationship with God. Now as we talk about the last six, see if you can figure out what relationship they're about.

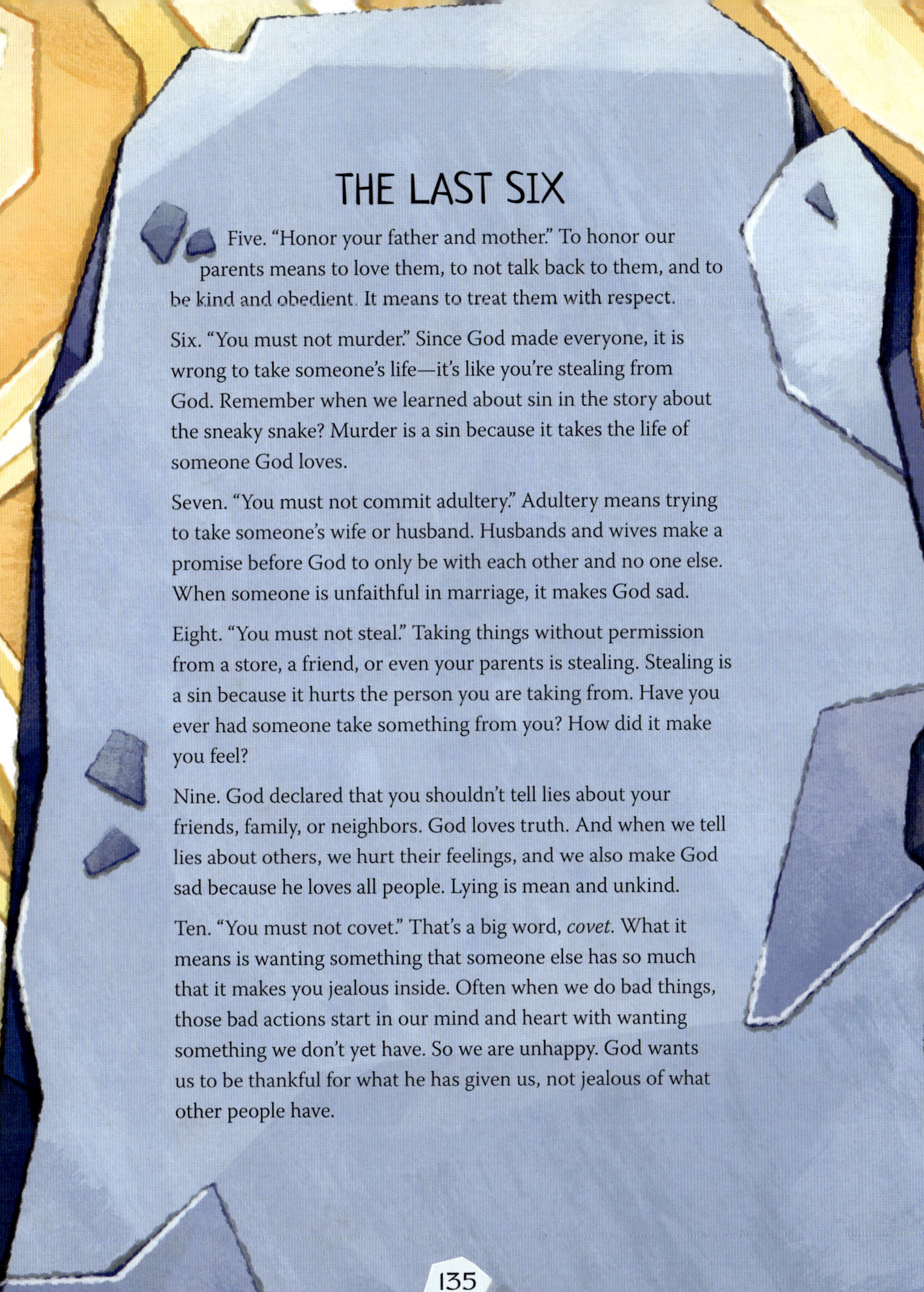

THE LAST SIX

Five. "Honor your father and mother." To honor our parents means to love them, to not talk back to them, and to be kind and obedient. It means to treat them with respect.

Six. "You must not murder." Since God made everyone, it is wrong to take someone's life—it's like you're stealing from God. Remember when we learned about sin in the story about the sneaky snake? Murder is a sin because it takes the life of someone God loves.

Seven. "You must not commit adultery." Adultery means trying to take someone's wife or husband. Husbands and wives make a promise before God to only be with each other and no one else. When someone is unfaithful in marriage, it makes God sad.

Eight. "You must not steal." Taking things without permission from a store, a friend, or even your parents is stealing. Stealing is a sin because it hurts the person you are taking from. Have you ever had someone take something from you? How did it make you feel?

Nine. God declared that you shouldn't tell lies about your friends, family, or neighbors. God loves truth. And when we tell lies about others, we hurt their feelings, and we also make God sad because he loves all people. Lying is mean and unkind.

Ten. "You must not covet." That's a big word, *covet*. What it means is wanting something that someone else has so much that it makes you jealous inside. Often when we do bad things, those bad actions start in our mind and heart with wanting something we don't yet have. So we are unhappy. God wants us to be thankful for what he has given us, not jealous of what other people have.

Did you notice what relationships God talks about in the last six commandments? Yes, it's about our relationships with people.

These are hard rules to follow, don't you think?

Why would God give such a difficult list of rules? These commands show us just how much we need God. On our own, we cannot love God well or treat others with love. It's not easy living in the light. We need his help because sometimes choosing darkness is easier.

Israel struggled with the Ten Commandments, just like we do. They welcomed the rules, but it was never easy to follow them. But God still had a plan to rescue all of us from that struggle.

John Reflects

When Jesus was on earth, he summed up the Ten Commandments in a simple way. He said, "The most important commandment is this: 'Listen, O Israel! The Lord our God is the one and only Lord. And you must love the Lord your God with all your heart, all your soul, all your mind, and all your strength.'" See how Jesus' words relate to the first four commandments? It's all about loving God with everything inside us.

Then Jesus added, "The second is equally important: 'Love your neighbor as yourself.'" Isn't it amazing that one simple rule summarizes the last six commandments?

God gave us these rules so that we can live in the bright light. To live in the light is to make the kinds of decisions that make God smile and help people know him. To live in darkness is to lie, cheat, hurt people, and steal. Doing things like that makes us feel bad, and like Adam and Eve in the garden, we hide after we sin. Instead, living in the light means we treat people with kindness because God made each and every person—even the bullies we meet. And even though the way of kindness is not always easy, it's the better way.

THE LIGHT MOMENT

God created ten rules to help our world run smoothly: the Ten Commandments. At Mount Sinai, he gave them to the Israelites so they could be his special people. Four rules are about our relationship with God, and six are about our relationships with people. These rules help us live in God's bright light.

Questions for Conversation

Which commandment is the easiest for you to follow? Why? And which one is the most difficult for you? Why?

What do you think it means to live in God's light? How do the commandments help you do that?

Prayer

Jesus, thank you for helping me obey you and live in the light. Thank you for perfectly obeying all the commandments and teaching me how to love you and love others. Amen.

WHEN THE SUN STOOD STILL

God Is More Powerful than the Sun

(JOSHUA 2–6, 10)

Before I started following Jesus, I'd wake up very early every morning while darkness still hung over the earth. My dad, brother, and I would go to our boat to prepare to fish. That was our job—we were fishermen. Every single morning, the sun peeked over the horizon, lighting up the entire sky. It traveled overhead during the day, and by nighttime, it set with brilliant oranges and pinks and yellows.

Have you seen a sunrise or a sunset? They're beautiful, aren't they? We can count on the sun rising and setting each day because that's how God designed our world to work. But did you know there was one time when the sun stopped in the middle of the sky? It all happened because God answered a prayer with a powerful miracle.

READY FOR THE PROMISED LAND

After God gave Israel the Ten Commandments, he also gave them what we call the Law—a big book about all God's ways that taught Israel how to love and obey him. The Law would help Israel follow God even when they were confused or scared. God also directed Israel to create a special box called the Ark of the Covenant. They covered the box in gold and treated it with respect because this was where God's presence would be. Whenever they saw the Ark, they would remember that God was with them.

Moses told Israel to always obey God because God knew what was best and loved them most. **Many years later, Moses grew very old, and he died. Israel needed a new leader, so God called a man named Joshua.** God said to Joshua, "Be strong and courageous! Do not be afraid or discouraged. For the Lord your God is with you wherever you go."

Joshua needed to be strong and courageous because God had an important job for him to do. You see, after wandering and waiting in the desert for forty whole years and hearing all about God's ways, **Israel was finally ready to go to the Promised Land!**

The Promised Land was the land God had promised to Abraham all those years ago. Abraham's family had grown to a giant family, just as God had said. And now, they could go into the land God had prepared for them. Hooray! Everyone packed up their bags and strapped on their sandals. They couldn't wait to come home to their very own land.

RIVER CROSSING

The Israelites sang and danced and skipped as they approached the Promised Land. But when they arrived, a large, flowing river blocked the path right where they needed to go. The water rushed too fast for them to swim, and no bridges went over the river. How would they get across?

Israel had needed to cross some water before—do you remember the Red Sea? God parted that great sea for the Israelites, and God could make a way for his people to cross this river as well.

And guess what? That's exactly what he did. God made the river stop flowing, and every single person walked across on dry land. Israel sang and danced and skipped again. If God could do this miracle for them, settling into their new homeland would surely be full of miracles too.

ENTERING THE LAND

There was just one problem. God's enemies lived in the Promised Land. **Everywhere Israel turned, they found people who did not love God or walk in his light.** Israel had to defeat God's enemies so they could live in the land. That's why God told Joshua to be strong and brave. God knew Joshua would have to go into battle against God's enemies, and God promised he would be with Joshua.

How would you feel having the all-powerful God of the universe on your team? Pretty good, right? Joshua and Israel had the best weapon of all: God. He could deliver them from their enemies—they just had to trust him.

JERICHO

Israel came to the first city full of angry, mean enemies. It was called Jericho and had tall walls that no one could climb over or knock down. Before the Israelites crossed the Jordan, Joshua had sent out spies to see what Jericho was like so Israel could defeat them. In the city there was a woman named Rahab who loved God. Rahab helped the spies escape, and the spies promised God would save her and her family since she had saved the spies.

After the spies reported back to Joshua, God gave Joshua a plan. And this plan seemed silly. Instead of attacking Jericho with swords and arrows, Israel marched around the city once a day for seven days. The Ark of the Covenant went first to show the people God was with them, and the warriors followed. God's enemies thought the Israelites were crazy. Who fought a city by walking around it?

On the last day, Israel marched around seven times, the priests blasted their horns, and all the soldiers shouted.

At first, nothing happened.

But then, *BOOM!* The walls of the city trembled. The stones shook and fell apart, crumbling so that Israel could swarm the city and defeat God's enemies. God did a miracle once again! Israel took control of Jericho, and Rahab and her family joined Israel.

A MIRACLE AND AN ANSWERED PRAYER

Israel ventured deeper into the Promised Land, fighting God's enemies along the way. Sometimes, they trusted God, as they had done in Jericho, and God strengthened them to win their battles. But other times, they disobeyed God by thinking they could win all by themselves, and their enemies defeated them.

One time, an evil king rallied many other kings to create a large army to fight Israel. Joshua could have been afraid, but God said to him, "Do not be afraid of them for I have given you victory over them. Not a single one of them will be able to stand up to you."

And God was right! He made Israel's enemies panic so they fought poorly. And then he sent hail on the enemy armies, which hurt them even more. Israel still needed to fight them in battle, but God prepared the way for them to win.

Joshua trusted God and believed he needed God to help him, so he prayed, "God, please let the sun stop moving in the sky so we have more time to defeat your enemies."

God listened to Joshua's prayer and answered him. **God stretched out his arm and kept the sun from sinking over the horizon. It stayed put all day long until Israel won the battle. Once again, the darkness could not defeat God or his people.**

John Reflects

God is so powerful, isn't he? He can stop up rivers, knock down walls, and hold the sun in the sky. These stories remind me of Jesus. He is powerful too. He calmed storms, healed people, and walked on water. Why do you think God does so many powerful miracles?

He performs miracles to show us his power and his love. Everything he did in these stories was to protect his people from harm because he loved them. He answered Joshua's prayer because he loves to hear and answer his people's prayers. That means he loves to hear and answer your prayers too.

THE LIGHT MOMENT

God called Joshua to lead the Israelites into the Promised Land. But the land was full of people who did not love God or walk in his light. As Israel fought their enemies, God kept the sun from going down all day long, until Israel won the battle. His strength is greater even than the sun.

Questions for Conversation

What would you do if the sun stayed shining for longer than a day?

God wants to hear and answer your prayers.
What do you want to pray to God about right now?

Prayer

God, you are powerful over everything, including the darkness. I know that you know what's best and love me perfectly. Please hear and answer my prayers. Amen.

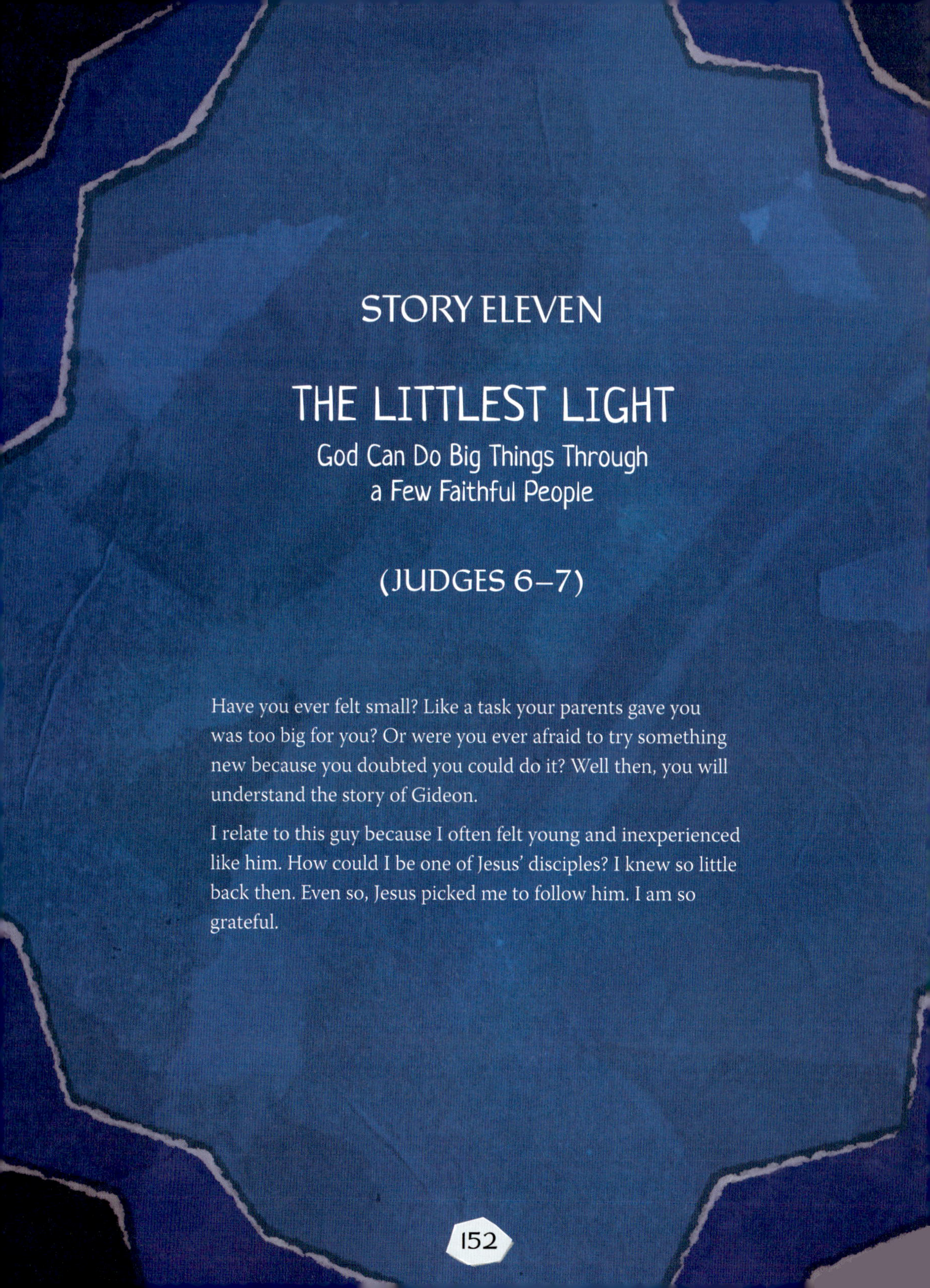

STORY ELEVEN

THE LITTLEST LIGHT

God Can Do Big Things Through a Few Faithful People

(JUDGES 6–7)

Have you ever felt small? Like a task your parents gave you was too big for you? Or were you ever afraid to try something new because you doubted you could do it? Well then, you will understand the story of Gideon.

I relate to this guy because I often felt young and inexperienced like him. How could I be one of Jesus' disciples? I knew so little back then. Even so, Jesus picked me to follow him. I am so grateful.

THE PROMISED LAND

Gideon's story starts after Joshua led the nation of Israel to the Promised Land. They made their home in the land full of honey (bees!) and milk (goats and cows!). But there was still so much to do. Even though God had warned the nation to follow only him, they were quick to chase after the gods of the land, choosing to worship lifeless statues (idols) rather than the God who had rescued them from the powerful Egyptians.

This era of history is called the time of the judges. This was before Israel had kings, so the rulers of the people were like the judges who sit in a courtroom (only their courtrooms were typically under trees or in tents). The judges helped people solve all sorts of problems. **Meanwhile, the people continued to do whatever they thought was right, and darkness crept in again.** They ignored the Ten Commandments, and they often took things into their own hands.

THE MEAN MIDIANITES

This disobedience hurt God. He allowed the Israelites to be raided by a tribe called the Midianites, a people who were cruel and mean and the worst kind of bullies you can imagine. The Israelites were so scared of Midian that they scoured the area for safe hiding places—in the crags of mountains and in musty underground caves and in abandoned buildings.

The people were so hungry that they risked planting crops, but the tribes around them trampled the new plants—they also took all their sheep, goats, cows, and donkeys. Seated on high camels, the Midianites looked down on the people of God. They were strong and muscular, and they didn't care that God's people were starving.

ISRAEL CRIES OUT

"Help us," the Israelites cried out to God.

God answered in a surprising way. The angel of the Lord (God himself!) sat underneath a giant tree in a place called Ophrah.

Nearby, Gideon beat wheat grains, separating grain from the grassy stalk. He worked hidden from sight in a hole in the ground, afraid that if the Midianites saw him, they'd take away all his grain.

MIGHTY HERO

The angel of the Lord interrupted Gideon's quiet, secretive work. "Mighty hero," he said. "The Lord is with you!"

You would think Gideon would be encouraged by such a greeting, but instead he challenged the angel. "If the Lord is with us, why has all this happened to us?"

Have you ever asked God that question? Have you ever felt sad that God didn't seem to be helping you when you struggled?

Gideon continued. "But now the Lord has abandoned us and handed us over to the Midianites."

The angel of the Lord turned toward him. **"Go with the strength you have, and rescue Israel from the Midianites. I am sending you!"**

GIDEON'S FEAR

Gideon shook inside. He said, "But Lord, how can I rescue Israel? My clan is the weakest in the whole tribe of Manasseh, and I am the least in my entire family!" He felt unable to do such a scary, impossible thing, so to stall, he made a meal of braised meat and pita bread for the angel. When the angel touched it, everything burst into flames.

"I'm doomed!" Gideon shouted. "I can't believe I've seen the angel of the Lord. What will happen to me now?"

"Do not be afraid. You will not die," the angel of the Lord reassured him. Then he told Gideon what to do next. He must find his father's altar to a god named Baal and wreck it, replacing it with memorial stones to God.

He had to tear down his own father's shrine! But you know what? Gideon took ten servants and did exactly what God said—except he was afraid of his father and the people, so he cut down the Baal altar at night.

Like Gideon feared, the people did not like that he had torn down the place where they worshiped a fake god. They hollered at Joash, Gideon's father. "Bring out your son," they demanded. "He must die."

Joash hollered back, "If Baal truly is a god, let him defend himself and destroy the one who broke down his altar!"

WAR IS NEAR

Later the people of the east and another fierce tribe called the Amalekites joined Midian so they could gang up on Israel.

Even though Gideon felt small, God gave him power. Still, Gideon wanted a sign that God would help him against this gigantic army. He gathered a fleece of wool (a thick pile of fluffy sheep hair) and put it on the ground. He told God that if the fleece was wet in the morning but the ground was dry, he would know God would help him.

Sure enough, that's exactly what happened.

But still, Gideon was afraid. So he changed the test. If the wool was dry but the ground was wet, then God would help him. And that's what happened.

THE SMALLEST ARMY

Gideon got up early and gathered his troops on the mountaintop above where the battle would be fought. But God said he had too many men! This made no sense to Gideon because it's always better to have more troops. God told Gideon to say, "Whoever is timid or afraid may leave this mountain and go home." Of the men who were there, twenty-two thousand went home, leaving ten thousand who were not afraid to fight.

But God said there were still too many troops! This time, Gideon took the ten thousand to the brook so he could watch how the men drank water. Most of them lapped the water like a dog, but three hundred cupped water in their hands and drank. God chose the men who cupped the water!

SPYING

The Midianite camp spread out below them like thousands upon thousands of sleeping grasshoppers, too many to count. God told Gideon and his companion Purah to spy on them that night. They snuck up on two men. One of them described a dream of a barley loaf rolling down over the Midianite camp, knocking everything flat. His friend said, "Your dream can mean only one thing—God has given Gideon son of Joash, the Israelite, victory over Midian and all its allies!"

This gave Gideon courage.

THE PLAN

He bowed down and thanked God, then shouted to his three hundred men, "Get up! For the Lord has given you victory!" Dividing the men into three groups of one hundred, he did something surprising that night, handing each a ram's horn, a clay pot, and a flaming torch. He instructed the men to wait for his signal, then blow the horns, smash the pots, and reveal the torches.

They circled above the sleeping men, each with their horn, pot, and torch. At last, at Gideon's signal, they shouted, "A sword for the Lord and for Gideon!" They smashed their pots, revealing the flaming torches inside. The Midianites looked up, seeing what they thought was a giant army all around. They panicked, then fought each other. Some ran away, terrified.

And that's how God freed the Israelites from the angry grip of the Midianites—with a scared man named Gideon whose strength and faith God increased. **Maybe he felt insignificant, like the torch hidden in a clay pot. But as he smashed the pot, the light became brilliant against the night sky.**

John Reflects

So whenever you feel like your light is small, remember the story of Gideon, the least of the smallest tribe of Israel. Remember how God shaved down his army to three hundred men and how those men defeated thousands upon thousands of Midianites with horns, pots, and torches. It's a miracle—and God was the one who fought for and through Gideon.

THE LIGHT MOMENT

In the time of the judges, darkness crept in again, but the angel of the Lord sent Gideon to rescue Israel, despite his fear. With only three hundred men and some flaming torches, Gideon's army defeated the Midianites. Gideon's light became brilliant as God increased his strength and faith.

Questions for Conversation

Why do you think Gideon put a fleece on the ground and asked God twice about whether he should face Midian? Have you ever wanted God to clearly show you what he wanted you to do next?

When was a time you felt scared and God helped you through that scary time? What happened?

Prayer

Jesus, when I feel small, will you help me? I don't like being afraid. But I know you love to help people who are scared, so please help me. Amen.

FROM LOSING IT ALL TO GAINING EVERYTHING

God Provides for His People

(RUTH 1–4)

I used to think some people were too far away from God to follow him. But the story of Ruth shows us the opposite is true. Anyone can love God, even people who used to disobey him. Even more, this story points to how God provides for his people, and how he has a plan for them, even when they can't see it.

THE LAND OF GOD'S ENEMIES

There once was a land near Israel where God's enemies lived. It was called Moab. The people of Israel avoided Moab as much as they could, and they didn't like the people from there because they had once hurt the Israelites. In Israel's eyes, it was an evil land with evil people.

But this story's hero comes from the land of Moab. You know why? **Because anyone can choose to trust God—even people who were once his enemies.**

During the time of the judges, a man called Elimelech, his wife, Naomi, and their two sons decided to move away from Israel. There was a terrible famine in the land, so they left looking for food. They found it in the land of Moab and settled down there.

The family lived in Moab for a long time—so long that their sons grew up and got married to women from Moab. They were called Ruth and Orpah, and they loved their husbands and their husbands' parents very much. But before long, tragedy struck. The man and his two sons died, leaving Naomi, Ruth, and Orpah all alone. They cried and cried. They missed their husbands, and they were scared about the future.

MONEY, FOOD, PROTECTION

You see, back in Naomi, Ruth, and Orpah's time, if a woman was all alone without a husband, she had no money, no food, and no protection. It was also very important back then for wives to have babies, especially baby boys, so their families could continue to grow. Ruth and Orpah had no babies and no husbands, so if they wanted to be safe, they would need to get married again.

Ruth and Orpah wiped the tears from their eyes. "What will we do?" they asked Naomi.

Naomi gave her daughters-in-law a big hug. "We will go back to my hometown. I heard there is food there again. My family will help us."

So the three women packed their bags and set off on the winding road back to Israel. On the way, Naomi stopped her two daughters-in-law. She loved them very much, and she knew her people might not like Ruth and Orpah because they were from Moab—the land of God's enemies. She wanted them to be protected, so she said, "Go back to your mothers' homes. And may the Lord reward you for your kindness to your husbands and to me."

"No," they said. "We want to go with you to your people."

"There's nothing for you in my land. How will you find husbands in Israel when you're from a place they don't like at all? No, you should go home and leave me behind. If you follow me, you'll give up everything."

Tears streamed down Ruth's and Orpah's faces. Orpah hugged Naomi and went back to Moab, but Ruth held onto her mother-in-law with all her might.

RUTH'S BRAVE CHOICE

Naomi said, "Follow Orpah! She's going back to her hometown. You should do the same."

But Ruth refused, and she said something remarkable: "Don't ask me to leave you and turn back. Wherever you go, I will go; wherever you live, I will live. Your people will be my people, and your God will be my God."

Ruth made a brave choice. **She decided to follow Naomi wherever she went. But most of all, she chose to follow God and walk in his light.** She used to be a Moabite—an enemy of God. Now, she obeyed God, and **God had a special plan for Ruth.**

Ruth and Naomi returned to Israel right in time for the harvest. Do you think that was a coincidence? No way! God made sure they arrived at the perfect time so his special plan for Ruth could start unfolding.

GOD'S IMPORTANT RULE

God made an important rule in the Law back when Moses led Israel. He said if any people needed food in Israel, they could follow harvesters and pick up the extras. God wanted everyone to be taken care of, so he added rules about helping the poor and needy so his people would understand his heart. God cares so much about every person, and he wants his people to care about others too.

Ruth knew about God's important rule. She and Naomi needed food, so Ruth woke up early in the morning, before the sun peeked over the horizon. She went to a field in the middle of harvest and followed after the harvesters, picking up the leftover grain.

RUTH MEETS BOAZ

Ruth ended up in a field owned by one of Naomi's relatives. To Ruth, it seemed like an accident. But was it? No way! God made sure Ruth ended up in this field at this time. It was all a part of his special plan.

The owner of the field was Boaz, and he loved God. He noticed Ruth and asked his workers, "Who is that young woman over there? Who does she belong to?"

"That's Ruth," they said, "She came back from Moab with Naomi."

Boaz could have told Ruth to go away—she was from the land of God's enemies, after all. But because Boaz loved God, he also knew God's heart. He could take care of Ruth, and that's exactly what he did.

He told Ruth, "Stay in my fields and take as much food as you need. I'll make sure you're safe. I know all about how you followed Naomi here to a new place. You are brave and kind! May the Lord bless you for what you've done."

Ruth smiled and thanked him. By the end of the day, she had so much food in her arms that they ached. When Naomi saw how much grain Ruth had gathered and heard how Boaz had helped her, she rejoiced. She encouraged Ruth to keep working in Boaz's fields, and so Ruth did. Ruth and Naomi's bellies never grumbled—they had all the food they needed.

GOD PROVIDES FOR RUTH, NAOMI, AND THE WORLD

They still had a problem, though. Because neither of them had husbands, they still had no protection and no way to have a baby to keep their family going. Then, Naomi had a great idea. What if Ruth and Boaz got married? Then Ruth and Naomi would be protected, and maybe Ruth could have a baby!

Naomi told her idea to Ruth. "Go ask Boaz if he will marry you. Then you can be protected."

Ruth agreed, and she asked Boaz if he would marry her. He said

yes! **Ruth and Boaz got married, and they had a baby boy. They named the boy Obed.** And guess what? Obed grew up and had a son named Jesse, and Jesse grew up and had a son named David. David became the king, and many, many, many years later, his family had the most amazing descendant—Jesus. God used a woman who used to be from the land of his enemies to provide the entire world with the Savior.

John Reflects

Ruth's story shows that anyone—even an enemy of God—can love him and follow him. And it reminds me that even when all hope seems lost, God always has a plan. His light will break through the darkest circumstances. For Ruth, God provided food, protection, and a family. For us, God provided the Light of the World—Jesus, our Savior—through Ruth's family.

THE LIGHT MOMENT

Ruth followed Naomi to a far-off land—but most of all, she chose to follow God and walk in his light. And God had a special plan for her. She married Boaz and had a baby boy named Obed—one of the ancestors of Jesus.

Questions for Conversation

Have you ever wondered how God's light would break through in a hard circumstance? What happened?

How did God take care of Ruth and Naomi? How has God taken care of you? Who is someone you could help, just like God has helped you?

Prayer

God, I believe you can take care of me, even though things seem dark. Please help me today. Thank you for always having a plan. Amen.

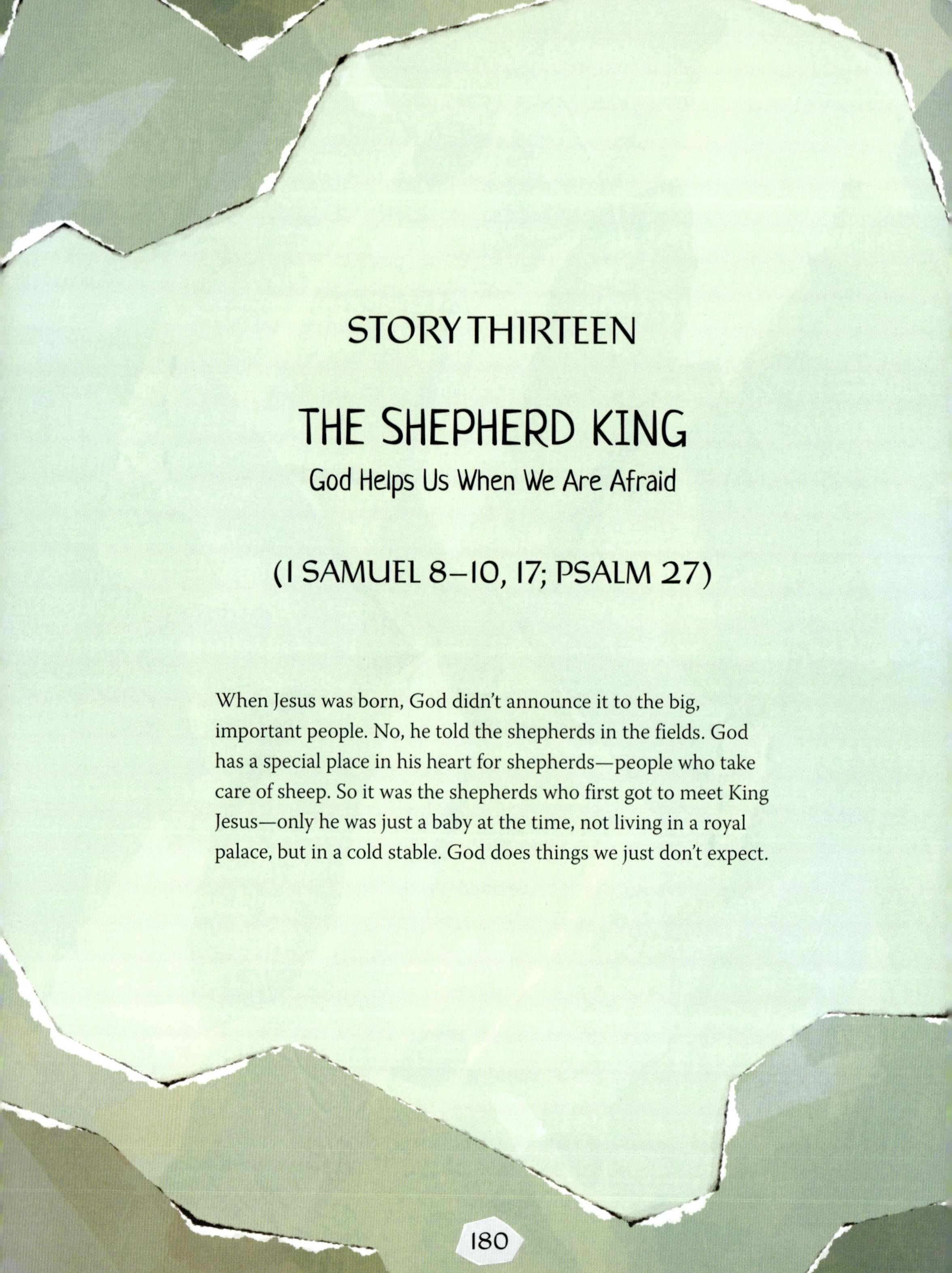

STORY THIRTEEN

THE SHEPHERD KING

God Helps Us When We Are Afraid

(1 SAMUEL 8–10, 17; PSALM 27)

When Jesus was born, God didn't announce it to the big, important people. No, he told the shepherds in the fields. God has a special place in his heart for shepherds—people who take care of sheep. So it was the shepherds who first got to meet King Jesus—only he was just a baby at the time, not living in a royal palace, but in a cold stable. God does things we just don't expect.

WE WANT A KING

Remember what I told you about the time of the judges? God was Israel's king, but he used judges to help solve the problems of the people. That setup happened for a really long time. God promised to be the shepherd king of Israel, to gently tend to the people, feed them, and protect them from harm.

The problem was that the people looked around at all the other nations and were mad. Remember the last commandment about coveting—about wanting what other people had? All the other nations had powerful kings, but Israel didn't. **So the people decided God wasn't enough for them—instead they wanted a real-life, human king to rule them.** This broke God's heart.

Still, he answered their complaints. A big, tall, handsome man named Saul became the king of Israel—but he only partially loved God. Mostly, he loved himself. And he didn't always consult God on what would be the best thing to do.

PHILISTINES!

During the reign of Saul, something awful happened. The strong, angry Philistines faced the Israelites. They stood tall on one hill, facing the Israelite army on the other hill. The Valley of Elah sat between them.

One day a Philistine giant named Goliath charged into the valley. He was over nine feet tall—tall enough that his head might bump your ceiling!

On his head sat a heavy bronze helmet. On his chest he wore a bronze coat of chain mail which weighed 125 pounds—as much as a washing machine. On his legs he sported bronze leg armor. He carried a heavy bronze javelin (a short spear meant for throwing), which was heavier than a tree trunk. And the head of the spear was iron, weighing more than a baby—fifteen pounds. Ahead of him walked his armor-bearer, carrying a broad shield.

Goliath sneered at the people of God. Maybe he even growled like a wolf. He pulled in a mighty breath, then shouted, "I am the Philistine champion, but you are only servants of Saul. Choose one man to come down here and fight me!"

No one answered him. The Israelites were terrified of this angry giant.

Goliath spit at the ground. "If he kills me, then we will be your slaves. But if I kill him, you will be our slaves! I defy the armies of Israel today! Send me a man who will fight me!"

Saul said nothing. Neither did his army. They had no response. No one was brave or stupid enough to face such a muscular, tall man.

Goliath paraded in front of the fear-filled Israelite army for forty days. Every morning and every night, he strutted, spewed taunting words, and harassed the people. Still, no one did anything.

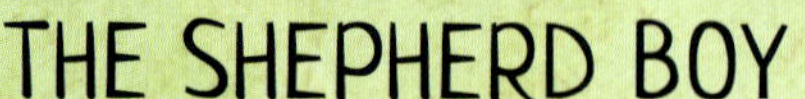

THE SHEPHERD BOY

During this time, David, the youngest of Jesse's seven sons, tended the sheep while his older brothers fought in the army. One day Jesse sent David to the front lines to bring his brothers cheese and provisions. "See how your brothers are getting along, and bring back a report on how they are doing," Jesse told his son.

David left his sheep with another shepherd (you should never leave your sheep unattended!), and he made his way to the Valley of Elah just about the time Goliath stepped out to tease and taunt the Israelite army. David took note of Goliath's words, his heavy armor, and his stature, then he watched as the army ran away from the giant. He stopped one of the fleeing soldiers and asked what was going on.

"He comes out each day to defy Israel," the soldier said. "The king has offered a huge reward to anyone who kills him."

Angry about Goliath's taunts, David asked, "Who is this pagan Philistine anyway, that he is allowed to defy the armies of the living God?"

A TEASING BROTHER

Eliab, David's eldest brother, thought David was getting too big for his britches. He pulled him aside at the valley's edge, then said, "What are you doing around here anyway?"

David didn't answer. But inside he fumed. Why did Goliath get away with saying such awful things?

Eliab grabbed David's much-thinner arm. "What about those few sheep you're supposed to be taking care of? I know about your pride and deceit. You just want to see the battle."

David scowled. "What have I done now? I was only asking a question."

Brothers still have a hard time getting along, don't they?

A CONVERSATION WITH A KING

David ran toward the king, daring to approach royalty. He was much shorter than King Saul, not yet fully a man. "Don't worry about this Philistine," David told him.

Saul shook his head, then chuckled. "You're only a boy, and he's been a man of war since his youth."

But David kept pestering the king. He told him about taking care of his flock. "When a lion or a bear comes to steal a lamb from the flock, I go after it with a club and rescue the lamb from its mouth. If the animal turns on me, I catch it by the jaw and club it to death."

Saul stepped back. These were powerful stories.

"I have done this to both lions and bears, and I'll do it to this pagan Philistine, too, for he has defied the armies of the living God!" **He promised that God would rescue him from Goliath.**

David pestered Saul so much that he finally agreed to let David face Goliath. Saul was afraid David would be hurt or killed, so Saul gave David his own heavy armor. Unfortunately, the suit of armor was way too large for David. He couldn't run or fight in it. He took it off, handing it back to the king.

DAVID'S WEAPONS

Instead, David ran to a nearby stream. There, he picked up five smooth, rounded stones. He plopped them in the leather bag fastened on the side of his hip. With his shepherd's staff and sling in hand, and the five rocks in his pouch, he ran across the Valley of Elah to face Goliath.

What do you think David felt as he got closer and closer to the giant and his armor bearer?

David had little time to think about being afraid.

"Am I a dog that you come at me with a stick?" Goliath yelled. He made fun of David, then yelled some more.

But David felt God's powerful strength. He knew darkness could not overcome God's great light. He yelled back, "You come to me with sword, spear, and javelin, but I come to you in the name of the Lord of Heaven's Armies—the God of the armies of Israel."

Goliath grunted and growled. As he started toward David, the boy ran at full speed toward the giant man. In a quick motion, he pulled out one stone, placed it in his sling, then flung it at Goliath with such force that Goliath fell face down to the ground. When the Philistines saw this, they ran clear away. God delivered the Israelites from the might of the Philistines that day by the quick hand of David.

AFTER GOLIATH

You may know that David would eventually become king of all Israel, but he had to experience many sleepless nights and worries before that happened. King Saul, who had become jealous of David, often chased him and forced him to hide in caves and clefts of rocks.

After Saul died, David was no longer a young boy with a sling and some rocks. He had grown tall and strong, but he never forgot what he had learned as a shepherd. There, he found God to be good company. In those quiet moments, David wrote songs to God, loving him with music. And he learned how to care for people, just as he had tended his lambs.

When he was king, he was known as someone who had a heart that loved God more than anything else. He continued to write songs about God, light, and his help. Here is one of them:

> The Lord is my light and my salvation—so why should I be afraid? The Lord is my fortress, protecting me from danger, so why should I tremble? . . . I am confident I will see the Lord's goodness while I am here in the land of the living. Wait patiently for the Lord. Be brave and courageous. Yes, wait patiently for the Lord.

John Reflects

When you are afraid, remember David, the shepherd who became a king. If you follow David's line, you'll see that Jesus is one of David's descendants. Just like David, Jesus was someone who loved God so much, and he also was (and is) a Shepherd King. In fact, he told us disciples, "I am the good shepherd; I know my sheep, and they know me, just as the Father knows me and I know the Father. So I sacrifice my life for the sheep."

THE LIGHT MOMENT

The Israelites decided God wasn't enough for them—they wanted a real-life, human king. But it wasn't their king, Saul, who faced the giant Goliath—it was David, a young shepherd. David knew Goliath's darkness could not overcome God's light.

Questions for Conversation

Why is it so hard to stand up to a bully?
What do you think about David running right at Goliath? In what ways has God helped you be courageous against darkness, like David?

Who in your life is a good shepherd of animals? (Who takes good care of their animals?) And who do you know who is a good shepherd of people?

Prayer

Jesus, thank you that when I'm afraid, you shepherd me and take care of my worries. Help me to someday stand up to bullies, but with your help. Amen.

STORY FOURTEEN

THE WISEST REQUEST

God Gives us Wisdom

(1 KINGS 3, 6–8; PROVERBS 3–4)

Sometimes, I don't know the right choice to make. Have you ever felt that way? Sometimes it's easy to see if something is wrong, like stealing or lying or cheating. We have the Ten Commandments to help us know those things are wrong. But sometimes the choices are more difficult, like who should be our friends or how we should spend our time.

Because I follow Jesus, I want to be like him, which means I need to make good choices like he did. Jesus always did the right thing—he knew God's heart and God's ways. We call that wisdom. Jesus was the wisest person to ever walk the earth, but a long time before he came, there lived a king who had God's amazing wisdom too.

KING SOLOMON'S REQUEST

That king was Solomon, David's son. King David ruled over Israel for many years. He loved God with all his heart and ruled kindly. When he died, Solomon became king. He had watched his dad govern Israel all his life. David showed him how to obey God, care for the people as a shepherd, and stand strong against God's enemies.

When Solomon sat on his shining throne and put on his heavy golden crown, he knew he had a tremendous responsibility. Ruling a whole nation meant making a lot of decisions. **He wanted to know which choices would honor God.**

One night, as Solomon slept, God came to him in a dream. God said, "What do you want? Ask, and I will give it to you!"

What would you ask God for if he offered to give you anything you wanted?

What do you think Solomon asked for?

He could have asked for victory over his enemies. Or a palace full of gold. Or a name so famous that everyone in the world would know him.

But he didn't.

Instead, he replied, "Give me wisdom so that I can govern your people well and know the difference between right and wrong. How could I rule these people without your help?"

God loved Solomon's request because he enjoys giving wisdom to his people. **God's wisdom is the light that shows us where to go.** It makes God happy when his people want to know him and his ways. So he responded to Solomon, "I will give you what you asked for! I will give you a wise and understanding heart such as no one else has had or ever will have!"

SOLOMON SOLVES A MYSTERY

Solomon used the wisdom God gave him to make good decisions. One time, two moms argued over a baby. One mom said the baby was hers, but the other insisted the baby belonged to her. It was a tricky situation. Which woman was telling the truth?

Solomon needed God's wisdom to solve the mystery. Solomon remembered how much his mom loved him. She would never let anyone hurt him. Good moms like her protect their babies no matter what. He knew that the real mom would never let her baby fall into harm's way, so he tried an experiment.

He said, "Give me a sword. If I cut the baby in two, you will both have a baby."

Now, was Solomon *really* going to hurt the baby? No! And did he think hurting a baby was right? Not at all. It's never okay to hurt someone, especially a baby. But Solomon needed a way to know who the real mom was, and he knew the real mom wouldn't want her baby to be harmed.

One woman shrugged. "That's fine with me," she said.

But the other woman screamed, "No! Please don't hurt my baby. Give him to the other woman so he can live."

Who do you think was the real mom? The one who wanted the baby to live! Solomon solved the mystery using God's wisdom. He returned the baby to the real mom, and the baby was safe. God's wisdom saved the day.

GOD'S GIANT HOUSE

Solomon continued to use God's wisdom to build a giant house for God called the Temple. God gave specific instructions for building his house, and Solomon followed all of them. For years and years, God's people went to the Temple to worship God. Even Jesus went to the Temple when he was on earth.

GOD'S WAYS

Solomon also wrote down the wisdom God gave him. You can find his words in a book of the Bible called Proverbs. Proverbs tells us about good choices and bad choices—God's ways and evil ways. When we make good choices, or choose God's way, we choose the light. But when we make bad choices, we choose the darkness. Look at what Solomon wrote in Proverbs: "The way of the righteous is like the first gleam of dawn, which shines ever brighter until the full light of day. But the way of the wicked is like total darkness. They have no idea what they are stumbling over."

When we choose wisdom, it's like walking in the sunshine. You can see everything in front of you. But choosing to disobey God is like walking with a blindfold on, or like walking in the dark. You can't see anything, and you'll trip and hurt yourself. We should follow God's ways because his ways are good for us. His wisdom protects us, shows us right from wrong, and helps us.

If Solomon could talk to you today, do you know what he'd say? He'd say to choose God's wisdom. He wrote, "Trust in the Lord with all your heart; do not depend on your own understanding. Seek his will in all you do, and he will show you which path to take."

Wisdom means trusting God no matter what. It means believing his ways are best. It means making choices that make God smile. Using God's wisdom is like running around on a sunshiny day—we see the right way to go, we avoid tripping or stubbing our toes, and we get to enjoy God and his world.

John Reflects

We can be wise like Solomon too. Jesus' brother James wrote, "If you need wisdom, ask our generous God, and he will give it to you." It's true! You can find God's wisdom in the Bible, by asking people who love Jesus too, and by praying to God. If you ever wonder if something is right or wrong, you can ask God for wisdom. He will tell you which way to go, just like he did for Solomon.

THE LIGHT MOMENT

Solomon wanted to know which choices would honor God, so he asked for wisdom, and God gave it to him. He knew that God's wisdom is the light that shows us where to go. Solomon used God's wisdom to build a giant house for God. And he wrote down God's wisdom in the book of Proverbs.

Questions for Conversation

How do you feel when you can't see in the dark?
What makes being in the light better?

What do you do when you don't know the right choice?
How can you ask God for wisdom?

Prayer

God, thank you for giving me wisdom when I ask for it. Please help me be wise today so I can walk in your light. Amen.

THE LORD, HE IS GOD

God Is Powerful over His Enemies

(1 KINGS 17–19)

Wisdom takes a while to get. I know it's taken me a long time to figure out how to live my life and love God and other people well. Solomon, as you just read, had a lot of wisdom. Some of the kings who followed after him were also wise, but many of them chased after idols and were disobedient to God.

God sent prophets to tell the people and their leaders that they were not living wholeheartedly for the Lord. They pointed out how Israel could return to God and feel God's presence and peace. One of the most famous prophets was Elijah. In this story, we're going to learn about Elijah's showdown with those who followed a false god named Baal, who was terribly wicked.

NO RAINSTORMS

Let's start with some history. Did you know that the nation of Israel divided into two?

It split into a northern kingdom named Israel and a southern kingdom named Judah. So there were kings in both places. After many kings, a new king began to rule in the northern land of Israel. His name was Ahab, and he had a wife named Jezebel who made him worship the god Baal. She attempted to get rid of all the Lord's prophets.

That's where Elijah comes on the scene. **He's a pretty interesting person, full of God's light and God's power.** Ravens fed him. He provided food for a poor widow and raised her son back to life. He prophesied that rain would stop falling in the land—and what he said happened. This caused a severe famine, where no one had food.

King Ahab did not like the prophet Elijah. He blamed Elijah for the famine, and he wanted to harm him. One day, Elijah decided to meet with Ahab, even though the king wanted to hurt him. He approached the king.

"So," King Ahab said, "Is it really you, you troublemaker of Israel?"

"I have made no trouble for Israel," Elijah replied. He looked at Ahab, then said, "You and your family are the troublemakers, for you have refused to obey the commands of the Lord and have worshiped the images of Baal instead." He pointed to a nearby mountain. "Now summon all Israel to join me at Mount Carmel, along with the 450 prophets of Baal and the 400 prophets of Asherah, who are supported by Jezebel."

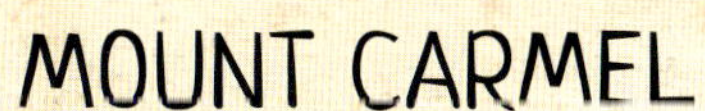

Ahab agreed, and all those prophets, 850 in all, gathered on Mount Carmel. The people of Israel followed too.

Elijah stood in front of the crowd. "How much longer will you waver, hobbling between two opinions? If the Lord is God, follow him! But if Baal is God, then follow him." He hoped someone would respond to this challenge, but no one said anything.

Elijah shook his head. He felt alone—the only one trying to help the people follow God. He instructed the prophets to find two bulls, then use one to sacrifice to their god, Baal, on an altar they had created. Elijah would sacrifice the second bull to the Lord on a different altar. They could add wood to the altar, but they could not set fire to it. "Then call on the name of your god," Elijah said, "and I will call on the name of the Lord. The god who answers by setting fire to the wood is the true God!"

BAAL'S ALTAR

Everyone agreed. Elijah told the prophets of Baal to go first. So they prepared the altar, piled wood all around it, and started hollering to their god. From morning to lunchtime, they shouted. "O Baal, answer us," they screamed. But no fire came. They danced and jumped and circled the altar.

Midday, Elijah teased them. "You'll have to shout louder, for surely he is a god!"

They shouted more.

"Perhaps he is daydreaming," Elijah scoffed. He said maybe Baal was too busy going to the bathroom. "Or maybe he is away on a trip, or is asleep and needs to be wakened."

They danced more, hoping that Baal would finally listen to them. They continued screaming and dancing until evening fell.

No god replied. No fire came.

GOD'S ALTAR

Elijah gathered the people around him. He repaired God's altar that the people had torn down. He hefted twelve big stones, one for each of Israel's tribes, and fashioned them into a new altar to God. Next, he took a shovel and dug a deep ditch all around the altar. He placed wood on the altar, prepared the bull, and pointed to a bystander. "Fill four large jars with water," he instructed, "and pour the water over the offering and the wood."

They did.

"Do the same thing again."

They obeyed.

"Now do it a third time!"

So they poured water all over the altar a third time. And now the water not only soaked the sacrifice and the wood, but it also filled up the trench Elijah had dug. The pile was sopping wet—no one could make a fire out of such a soggy mess!

ELIJAH'S PRAYER

In the evening, Elijah prayed, looking heavenward. "O Lord, God of Abraham, Isaac, and Jacob, prove today that you are God in Israel and that I am your servant. Prove that I have done all this at your command. O Lord, answer me! Answer me so these people will know that you, O Lord, are God and that you have brought them back to yourself."

In the next second, fire flew from heaven. It burned up the offering and the wood. It even destroyed the stones and the dust around it, then the fire licked up all the water in the trench.

Everyone fell on the ground with their faces in the dust. "The Lord—he is God! Yes, the Lord is God!"

They were amazed at the power of God and the utter weakness of Baal. **That's just how much stronger God's light is than darkness.**

RAIN PREDICTED

After this powerful showdown, Elijah told Ahab to eat and drink quickly because a storm would be coming soon. Ahab listened, and then he ate and drank.

Elijah returned with his servant to Mount Carmel and Elijah prayed, his face between his knees. He alerted the servant, "Go and look out toward the sea."

The servant ran there, but didn't see anything in the sky above the sea.

Elijah kept praying. He told the servant seven times to look at the sky above the sea!

On the seventh time, the servant said, "I saw a little cloud about the size of a man's hand rising from the sea."

"Hurry to Ahab," Elijah shouted, "and tell him, 'Climb into your chariot and go back home. If you don't hurry, the rain will stop you!'"

In a moment, the sky went from dazzling blue to dark as night. Wind swirled around, then rain pelted everyone and everything.

The rains had returned! And Baal's prophets had been humiliated.

John Reflects

Elijah's story shows us just how powerful God is. He can send fire from heaven that licks up water! But did you know that right after this amazing encounter, Elijah got really sad and tired? He was so afraid of Jezebel that he spent his time worrying and stressing. But God was kind to him, bringing him food and rest. And he spoke to him gently in a quiet breeze.

Have you ever experienced a high but then crashed afterward? I know I have—especially right after Jesus raised Lazarus (high!) but then was crucified (the worst low!) soon after. Life can be full of ups and downs. But God is kind. He knows what we need. He takes care of us and gives us strength.

THE LIGHT MOMENT

Elijah was a prophet full of God's light and God's power. The prophets of the false god Baal could not call down fire to light their sacrifice, but when Elijah called, fire flew from heaven and burned up the offering and the wood. That's just how much stronger God's light is than darkness.

Questions for Conversation

What do you think Elijah thought when God sent fire on his altar? How did he feel?

When have you felt sad or alone or tired this last month? How did God take care of you?

Prayer

Jesus, thank you for displaying such awesome power to the people and the prophets of Baal. Your fire from heaven overcame the darkest darkness! Amen.

STORY SIXTEEN

A LIGHT WILL SHINE

God Gives His People Hope

(ISAIAH 6, 9)

When you feel sad or scared or confused, what do you do? I try to talk to God about how I'm feeling, but sometimes I don't know what to do. God's people often feel this way. That's why God gives us a very special gift for those times. It's called hope. Hope means we trust in the true things God said will happen someday. We may not see it right now, but we will in the future.

There was a time when God's people really needed hope.

MEET THE PROPHETS

After the kingdom of Israel split in two (Israel in the north and Judah in the south), the people started disobeying God more and more. Sometimes a good king would help them remember God and his ways, but mostly the people kept choosing to ignore God. They thought their way was best. **So God sent leaders called prophets to help them obey God again.**

The prophets were God's messengers. They acted like God's mouth, talking for God and saying his words. We met one already—Elijah—but there were many, many more. Some of them had funny names, some of them did silly things, but all of them proclaimed God's words to people who were rebelling against God.

God saw all the ways his people were disobeying him, and it made his heart sad. God wanted his people to turn away from their sin and back to him—we call that repentance. Repentance happens when we stop disobeying God, ask for forgiveness, and obey him instead. God always forgives us when we repent. But if we keep on disobeying, we'll experience the sad consequences.

God pleaded with his people to come back to him because he loved them. But he also knew how difficult it was to stop disobeying. He knew what would happen—that they would keep messing up over and over again. They couldn't help it. They needed a Savior to rescue them from their sin.

GOD'S MESSAGE

So God gave the prophets a true but tough message:

"You've sinned, and you've messed up. You need to repent because if you don't, you'll experience the sad consequences. But don't worry—no matter what, **I am sending a Rescuer to save you.** You have hope."

Do you think the people liked hearing that message? How would you feel if you heard those words?

Israel and Judah bristled at God's message. They didn't like hearing they were wrong. So they were mean to many of God's prophets. In their eyes, it was easier to be mean than obey God. But God's messengers kept going, going, going. They persisted because they loved God and believed his words. They had hope.

ISAIAH'S CALL

One of those messengers was Isaiah. One day, he had an incredible dream. He saw God on his enormous throne. God's robe filled the entire room, and special angels with six wings each flew around the throne. They said, "Holy, holy, holy is the Lord of Heaven's Armies! The whole earth is filled with his glory!"

Have you heard the word *holy* before? It means that something is special, set apart, and perfect. When we call God holy, we're saying he deserves all our praise because he's different than us—he's perfect, good, powerful, wise, and kind. When the angels say he's "holy, holy, holy," that means he's *super-duper* holy—the most perfect in the entire universe.

Isaiah trembled when he heard the angels yell "holy, holy, holy" because he knew he was not holy at all. He had messed up before. He couldn't compare to how perfect God is! He cried out, "It's all over! I am doomed, for I am a sinful man."

God could have said, "You're right, Isaiah. You've messed up so much. You can't be near me. Go away!" But he didn't. Instead, he forgave him. Then he said, "I wonder who I can send as my messenger. Who will go share my message with my people?"

That must have been a scary moment for Isaiah. He didn't know what God would tell him to say. What if people didn't like the message? What if people were mean to him?

Even though he was nervous, Isaiah also loved God. He wanted to obey him. So he piped up. "Here I am," he said, "Send me."

HOPE FOR GOD'S PEOPLE

And God did. He gave Isaiah incredible messages that Isaiah then told God's people. Isaiah warned them that if they didn't obey God, they would experience the sad consequences. One of the big consequences Isaiah talked about was the exile. *Exile* is a fancy word for saying you're sent away from your home, and you can't come back. If Israel and Judah kept disobeying God, their enemies would defeat them and take them away from their homeland. They'd be stuck. That's sad, isn't it? Do you think they obeyed?

They didn't. And before long, their enemies defeated them and carried them off to foreign lands. How would you feel if you had to go away from home forever? Sad? Scared? Confused? God's people felt all those things. The exile made everything seem dark and hopeless. But remember—God's message didn't end at the sad consequences, did it?

God's message also had hope. He promised that one day Israel could go home again. Even more, a Rescuer was coming! Isaiah talked a lot about this Savior. He wrote, "The people who walk in darkness will see a great light. For those who live in a land of deep darkness, a light will shine."

Who do you think the Light is? **Who was going to come to shine light in the darkness?** Isaiah had no idea, but hundreds of years before Jesus came, he wrote about how Jesus would rescue the world, shining his light for all to see. All of Israel had hope that someday, their Rescuer would come.

PROPHECIES

Isaiah wrote more prophecies about Jesus than anyone. Prophecies are words from God about the future that someday come true. And guess what? Jesus fulfilled every single one of those prophecies! That's pretty amazing, isn't it?

But Isaiah didn't just write about Jesus—he talked about our future with God forever. **He said that someday, we won't need the sun anymore because God himself will be our light.** God will take away all the bad, evil things. He will make the earth brand new and peaceful—so peaceful that lambs and lions and little kids can be friends. Can you imagine a world like that?

John Reflects

I'm excited for our happy future with God someday. God always does what he says he'll do, which means the future he's promised will come true. After all, every single one of Isaiah's prophecies about Jesus happened, and God eventually restored the Israelites to their homeland, just as he said he would. God is trustworthy. When we're sad or scared or confused, we can remember that God's promises always come true. And the best promise of all is Jesus, the Light of the World.

THE LIGHT MOMENT

God sent prophets to the people. He pleaded with them to come back to him because he loved them. And he promised to send a Rescuer who would shine light in the darkness. One day, God himself will be our light.

Questions for Conversation

How would you feel if you saw God shining on his throne, like Isaiah did?

What do you think our happy future with God will be like? Will it be full of light or darkness?

Prayer

God, you are holy, which means you're perfect. I trust your promises. Thank you for giving me hope through Jesus. Amen.

STORY SEVENTEEN

THEY DIDN'T SMELL OF SMOKE

God Is With His People, Even in the Fire

(DANIEL 1–3)

No one really likes to be in exile. In exile you can't ever go home. You're stuck. When I was following Jesus wherever he walked, I didn't have a home either. It was difficult not having everything familiar near me, but I will never regret the adventure I had with Jesus.

This story takes place during the exile in a land called Babylon. It looks like you'd pronounce it "baby-lawn," but it's pronounced "babble-on." And it's where the nation of Israel found themselves after chasing idols and not following God. They had chosen to walk away from the light of God—but they hated where they ended up.

FOUR SPECIAL MEN

The king of Babylon had a very long name: Nebuchadnezzar. It's pronounced like this: "NEH-byoo-kuhd-NEHZ-er." He's the one who conquered the southern kingdom of Judah. He marched into Jerusalem and brought everyone back to Babylon. He ordered his chief of staff to gather some of the young noble men of Jerusalem to train as a part of his court. He wanted them to be strong, good-looking, healthy, smart, and wise. Four of those men were Daniel, Hananiah, Mishael, and Azariah. But the chief of staff gave them new Babylonian names: Belteshazzar, Shadrach, Meshach, and Abednego. See if you can say them!

The chief of staff wanted to have the four men eat rich, fattening foods, but Daniel (Belteshazzar) asked him if they could simply eat vegetables and water instead. Daniel and his friends wanted to honor God by keeping the diet taught in God's law. This worried the chief of staff because what if their diet made them less healthy? But the attendant agreed to a ten-day trial, and at the end of that time, those four men looked healthier than any of the other men who ate the rich foods. They also impressed King Nebuchadnezzar with their wisdom, and the king welcomed them into the royal service.

THE KING'S DREAM

One night, the king had a scary dream. He called all the magicians and astrologers of the land together and asked them to tell him his dream and what it meant. But he wouldn't tell them what the dream was, wanting them to prove their power. They panicked! One said, "No one on earth can tell the king his dream! And no king, however great and powerful, has ever asked such a thing of any magician, enchanter, or astrologer! The king's demand is impossible. No one except the gods can tell you your dream, and they do not live here among people."

The king stormed off. He did not like their excuses. He decided to kill all the wise men of the kingdom—a very harsh response.

But Daniel was wise. He decided to seek God. And God told him what the king's dream was. Daniel praised God, saying, "He reveals deep and mysterious things and knows what lies hidden in darkness, though he is surrounded by light. . . . You have told me what we asked of you and revealed to us what the king demanded."

Daniel rescued the wise men of the kingdom when he said, "Don't kill the wise men. Take me to the king, and I will tell him the meaning of his dream."

Daniel told the king he had dreamt of a frightening statue with a golden head, silver chest and arms, bronze thighs, and iron lower legs with feet made of iron and clay. A giant boulder had smashed the statue's feet so that it'd toppled to the ground and been obliterated—nothing left. Daniel then interpreted the dream, telling about four different kingdoms that would rule the world. The fourth kingdom, represented by the legs of iron and feet of clay and iron, would be divided and weak. God's Kingdom would crush all four kingdoms. Daniel said, "The great God was showing the king what will happen in the future. The dream is true, and its meaning is certain."

The king rewarded Daniel by letting him rule over the province of Babylon. Daniel asked that his three friends join him so they could rule together.

THE GOLDEN STATUE

Ninety feet is very tall. It would be like fifteen men standing on top of each other's shoulders, all the way to the sky. Can you imagine?

Now think about a statue that high. King Nebuchadnezzar made an enormous golden statue of himself that big—so gigantic that it touched the heavens. As soon as he made the statue, he sent messages to everyone in the land, particularly its leaders, so that they could come to the statue's dedication ceremony.

A herald shouted to all the people. He told them that as soon as they heard a horn, they had to bow down and worship the golden statue. "Anyone who refuses to obey," he shouted, "will immediately be thrown into a blazing furnace."

Everyone obeyed the order.

Except Shadrach, Meshach, and Abednego.

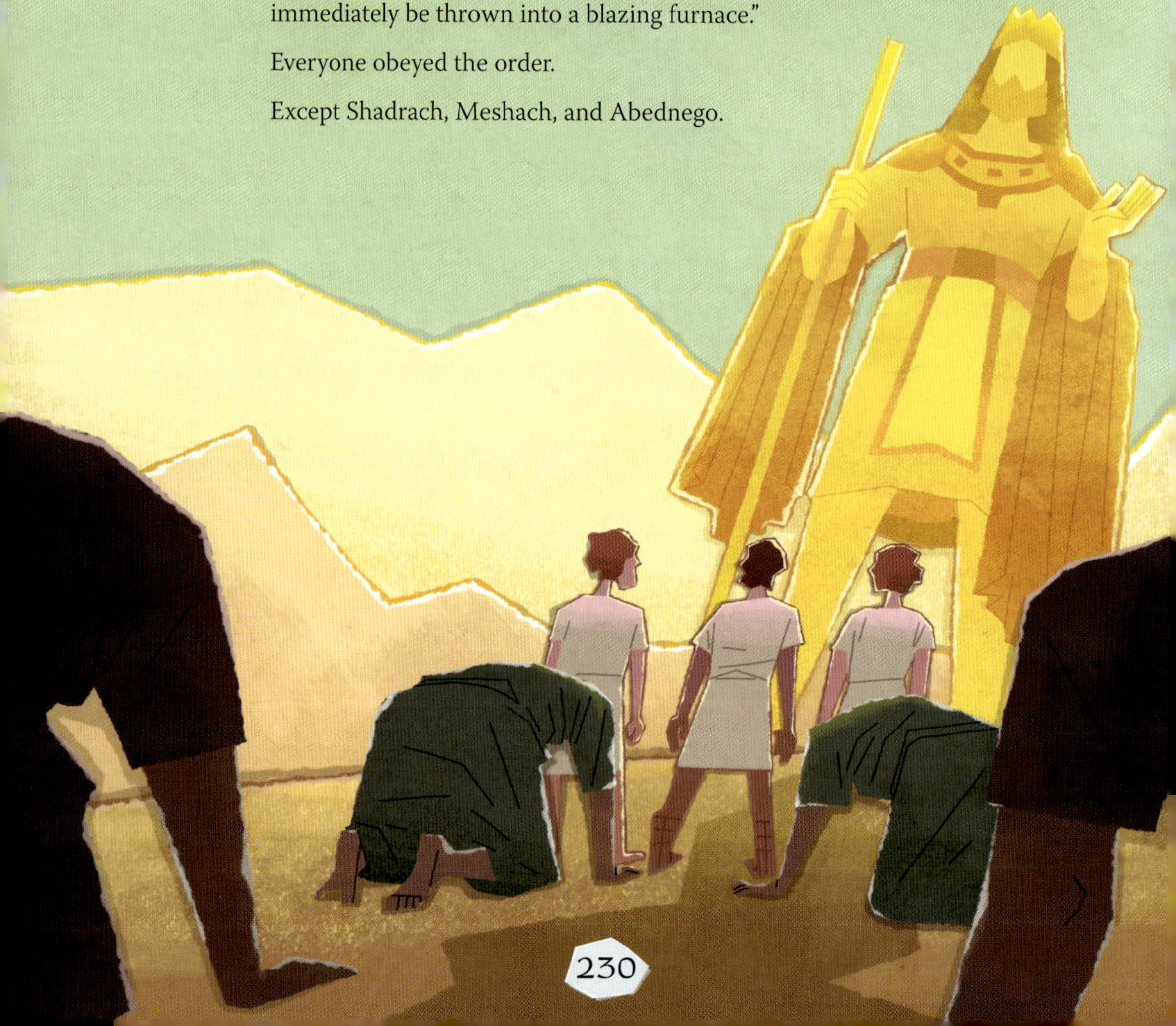

THE FIERY FURNACE

Then some astrologers told on the three wise men. This enraged King Nebuchadnezzar. He ordered that the three be brought in before him. He asked them if it were true that they wouldn't bow to the statue, and he gave them another chance to do so. He reminded them that if they refused, into a fiery furnace they'd go.

They said, "O Nebuchadnezzar, we do not need to defend ourselves before you. If we are thrown into the blazing furnace, the God whom we serve is able to save us." What bravery! They didn't seem to be worried about disobeying the king's crazy command. They continued, "He will rescue us from your power, Your Majesty. But even if he doesn't, we want to make it clear to you, Your Majesty, that we will never serve your gods or worship the gold statue you have set up."

As you can imagine, the king flew into a red-hot rage. He told the people in charge of the furnace to add more wood and make it seven times hotter than it had ever been before. **He ordered the biggest, burliest men to tie up the three friends, then throw them into the blazing room of fire.** The fire was so hot that the strong men were burned up when they pushed Shadrach, Meshach, and Abednego into the angry flames.

THE FOURTH MAN

But something surprising happened soon after.

King Nebuchadnezzar peered into the furnace. Instead of seeing three men, he noticed four. The three were no longer tied up. The fourth one, the king said, looked like a god—shiny and otherworldly. **The flames touched none of them, and they weren't being burned up.** The scene before him so startled the king that he yelled, "Shadrach, Meshach, and Abednego, servants of the Most High God, come out! Come here!"

They obeyed the king's order this time. Every noble person surrounding the king noticed that the three men were not singed by the fire. They still had full heads of unburnt hair, and their clothing was untouched. They didn't even smell like smoke.

This made the king praise the God of Shadrach, Meshach, and Abednego. He said, "There is no other god who can rescue like this."

John Reflects

Who do you think was the fourth person who stood in the flames with the three friends and protected them? Some believe it was Jesus before he came to the earth. Others think it was an angel. No matter who it was, the truth is, God can do miracles in impossible situations. And he loves to help those who are following him.

But did you catch what Shadrach, Meshach, and Abednego said before they went into the bright furnace? They said they would worship God even if he didn't save them from the flames. That's the kind of faith I want to have—to trust God even when things are scary and hard.

THE LIGHT MOMENT

God's people chose to walk away from his light—and they ended up in exile. But even in a faraway land, Daniel and his three friends served God and followed his laws. When the three friends wouldn't worship a statue of the king, he threw them into a fiery furnace. Yet God was with them in the fire, and they were not burned.

Questions for Conversation

How do you think Daniel felt when he told the king all about his dream? The magicians said it was impossible—that even gods didn't know what the dream was. What does this say about the awesomeness of our God?

How can walking in God's light help us become wise like Daniel?

Prayer

Jesus, when I am facing dark times, help me remember the stories of your faithful followers—Daniel, Shadrach, Meshach, and Abednego. Thank you for their example of trusting you even when it was hard. Amen.

STORY EIGHTEEN

THE LIGHT CAME INTO OUR WORLD

God's Plan Was Always to Send His Son

(MATTHEW 1–2; LUKE 1–2)

All people start out as babies. You did, and so did I. Jesus is God, so he could have come to Earth in many powerful ways. He could have taken a chariot of light from heaven and ridden into town. Or he could have flown in wearing a golden crown and flowing robe. But Jesus came the same way all of us do—as a baby. God's plan all along was for Jesus to be our Rescuer. But why did Jesus come that way?

MARY BELIEVED GOD

To find our answer, we need to meet Jesus' family. Let's start with his mom, Mary. Mary was young and engaged to Joseph, and they both loved God. One day, Mary sat by herself, and an angel appeared to her. He glowed so brightly it made her squint. He said to her, "Greetings, favored woman! The Lord is with you!"

Mary didn't know what to say. She was favored? God was with her? What did it all mean?

The angel could tell she was confused. "Don't be afraid, Mary," the angel told her, "for you have found favor with God! You will conceive and give birth to a son, and you will name him Jesus. He will be very great and will be called the Son of the Most High. The Lord God will give him the throne of his ancestor David. And he will reign over Israel forever; his Kingdom will never end!"

God's Rescuer, the Light of the World, was coming, and Mary would be his mom. What an amazing promise! But Mary saw a problem with the plan. She and Joseph weren't married yet, so how would she be able to have a baby?

She asked the angel, "How will this happen? Joseph and I aren't married yet."

"Don't worry, Mary. God can do anything! He will make the baby grow in you. It might seem impossible, but not for God. This is all part of his plan because this child will be special. He will be called the Son of God."

Mary's heart pounded. God was giving her a big responsibility. Could she do what he asked? She felt scared, but she believed God knew what was best. So she said, "I serve God, and I'll do what he asks me to do."

Mary became pregnant. Her belly swelled as little baby Jesus grew and grew. Mary praised God because everything he had said was coming true.

JOSEPH OBEYS GOD, TOO

Then Joseph found out and was confused. If Mary was being faithful to him, how could she have become pregnant before they were married? God noticed Joseph's confusion, so he came to Joseph in a dream.

He said, "Don't be afraid, Joseph. Mary is going to have a baby boy. This is all part of my plan to rescue the world! This baby will grow up and save people from their sins."

Joseph believed in God too, and he protected Mary while Jesus grew inside her. There's something else you need to know about Joseph. His great-great-greaaaaaat-grandpa (with even more greats) was King David, and King David's great-great-greaaaaaat-grandpa (with even more greats) was Abraham. Jesus came through this family because God promised he would—to David and to Abraham. God never forgets his promises, even the ones he made a really long time ago.

BABY JESUS ARRIVES

Then, the ruler of the empire decided he wanted everyone in his kingdom to go to their hometowns so they could be counted one by one. Joseph was from a place called Bethlehem, so he and Mary took a trip there to obey the ruler's command. But when they got there, oh no! **Mary was ready to have baby Jesus.** Where do you think they went to have the baby?

They tried to find a place to stay, but there was no room anywhere to be found. So they went to a stable—a place where animals eat and sleep. It was stinky and full of cows and goats and donkeys. Is that where you would expect a king to be born? No way! Kings are born in palaces, not barns.

But Jesus came into the world in a humble way. Do you know what being humble means? It means you think of others as more important than yourself. Jesus is the Light of the World, the king over everything. He's God! But he came as a baby in a smelly stable because we are more important to him than his royal throne.

Mary wrapped baby Jesus up all snuggly and put him in a manger—that's a large trough for animals to eat out of. She loved her little boy and praised God for keeping his promise to her.

THE RESCUER IS HERE

God wanted people to know his Son had been born. Who do you think God decided to tell about Jesus' birth? Important people? Powerful people? Smart people? He could have told them, but he had a different idea.

Some shepherds watched their sheep in the middle of the night. They could barely see each other in the dark, but then bam! An angel appeared all shiny and bright in front of them. "Don't be afraid!" he said. "I bring you the happiest good news for everyone. The Rescuer was born today in Bethlehem! Look for him: You will find a baby wrapped snugly in strips of cloth, lying in a manger."

Then the one angel became a big group of angels. **The sky lit up so brightly that it almost seemed like daytime. The angels all praised God and his Son, singing,** "Glory to God in highest heaven, and peace on earth to those with whom God is pleased."

The angels went back into heaven, and the shepherds jumped up, excited to meet the Rescuer sent by God. They ran as fast as they could and found Mary and Joseph, and baby Jesus in the manger, just as the angel had said.

Other visitors came to visit baby Jesus too. By following a shining star, some wise men from far away brought special gifts to Jesus—gifts that you would give to a king. Jesus is the King after all. A special kind of king who would rescue the whole world.

John Reflects

So why did Jesus come as a baby? Well, for a few reasons. It was always God's plan to send a Rescuer. Jesus came through the family of Abraham and David because God had promised that the Rescuer would. Jesus came humbly as a baby so he could be like us. He thinks of us as more important than his crown and royal throne. But even as a baby, he was the King, the Rescuer, and the Light of the World.

THE LIGHT MOMENT

A bright angel brought Mary news that God's Rescuer, the Light of the World, was coming to earth at last. When she was ready to have baby Jesus, he came in a humble way—in a smelly stable. To announce his birth, the angels praised God and the sky lit up like daytime. Jesus was born!

Questions for Conversation

How do you think Mary and Joseph felt when they heard baby Jesus was coming? What about the shepherds when they saw the bright, shining angels?

Are you glad Jesus came as a baby? What would you have done if you had gotten to meet him when he was in the manger?

Prayer

Jesus, thank you for coming as a baby to rescue us and bring light to the world. Help me to obey you like Mary and Joseph did. I love you, Jesus. Amen.

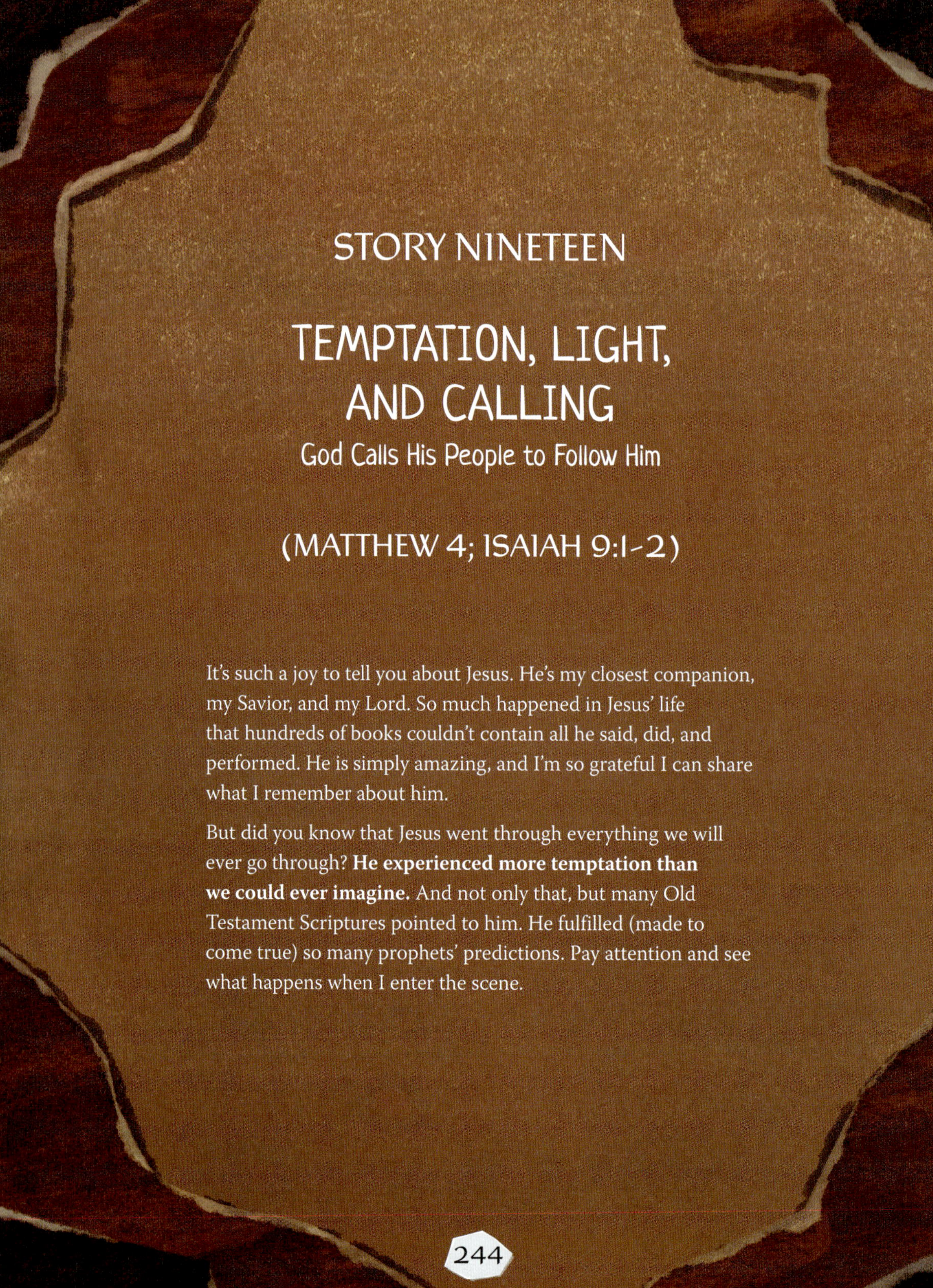

STORY NINETEEN

TEMPTATION, LIGHT, AND CALLING

God Calls His People to Follow Him

(MATTHEW 4; ISAIAH 9:1-2)

It's such a joy to tell you about Jesus. He's my closest companion, my Savior, and my Lord. So much happened in Jesus' life that hundreds of books couldn't contain all he said, did, and performed. He is simply amazing, and I'm so grateful I can share what I remember about him.

But did you know that Jesus went through everything we will ever go through? **He experienced more temptation than we could ever imagine.** And not only that, but many Old Testament Scriptures pointed to him. He fulfilled (made to come true) so many prophets' predictions. Pay attention and see what happens when I enter the scene.

40 DAYS

Jesus was thirty years old when he started his public ministry. But before he did miracles, taught the wisest words, and set people free from sin, the Holy Spirit led him into the deep wilderness, all alone. He didn't eat anything for forty days. Not figs, not bread, not meat, not even a bite of lettuce. He probably had limited water too.

Remember the sneaky snake in the garden? He's also known as the devil and Satan—and wouldn't you know, he showed up when Jesus was hungry and thirsty in the wilderness.

THREE TEMPTATIONS

Satan tempted Jesus. "If you are the Son of God, tell these stones to become loaves of bread." Satan pointed to a large pile of rocks.

Jesus had the power to do anything. But he knew that obeying Satan would be wrong. So he quoted from the Old Testament. "People do not live by bread alone," Jesus told the devil, "but by every word that comes from the mouth of God."

Satan wasn't finished tempting Jesus to sin, so he took him to Jerusalem. Together, they stood at the highest point of the Temple. You could see everywhere from there—certainly a large portion of the Promised Land.

The devil hissed, "If you are the Son of God, jump off! For the Scriptures say, 'He will order his angels to protect you. And they will hold you up with their hands so you won't even hurt your foot on a stone.'" Even the devil knew the words of the Bible. Maybe he thought Jesus would have to listen if he quoted Scripture.

But Jesus knew what the devil was up to. He simply said, "The Scriptures also say, 'You must not test the Lord your God.'"

The devil had one more scheme. He took Jesus to the very top of a gigantic mountain. In a quick moment, all the kingdoms of the world flashed before them both with lights and sparkle. What would it be like to own all the kingdoms? The devil said, "I will give it all to you if you will kneel down and worship me."

But Jesus knew that, as God, he already had all the kingdoms of this world. **Even more importantly, he was starting a new Kingdom—his!** Jesus had had enough of the devil's lies. Satan wanted Jesus to grab power for himself, but Jesus knew a true king loves and serves his people, so he said, "Get out of here, Satan. For the Scriptures say, 'You must worship the Lord your God and serve him only.'"

Satan slunk away, defeated.

Angels flew to Jesus, then took care of him.

LIGHT OF THE WORLD

John the Baptist was Jesus' cousin. He lived in the wilderness, where he ate bugs and honey and wore camel skins for clothing. John helped prepare people to meet Jesus by teaching them to be sorry for their sins. Remember Elijah, the prophet who had a showdown with the prophets of Baal and won? John the Baptist was a powerful prophet like Elijah.

After people said they were sorry for hurting God with their actions and words, John baptized them near the banks of the Jordan River. The Temple officials did not like this odd man, John, very much, especially since the people flocked to him, so they arrested him.

Shortly after that terrible arrest, John's cousin Jesus walked to Galilee, which is the region surrounding a great sea—the Sea of Galilee. First, he trekked to a little town named Nazareth, where he had grown up, then he stopped in Capernaum—a place that eventually became his home base. All this traveling reminded my friend Matthew of a prophecy by Isaiah in the Old Testament. Remember him? Isaiah had said, "In the land of Zebulun and of Naphtali, beside the sea, beyond the Jordan River, in Galilee where so many Gentiles live, the people who sat in darkness have seen a great light. And for those who lived in the land where death casts its shadow, a light has shined."

Do you see that last part? Jesus is the great Light of our world. **In a dark place, in this sin-shadowed world, Jesus shone brightly.**

CALLING

Jesus, the Light, sure did a lot of walking. And after the wilderness, he walked along the Sea of Galilee's shore. The sun shone high and sparkled over the lake. Offshore, in the distance, Jesus saw two men. They were fishermen who happened to be brothers—Simon (who would later be renamed Peter) and Andrew. Young and strong, they cast nets into the sea, hoping to catch many fish because that was the job they'd set out to do.

Jesus shouted from the shoreline, "Come, follow me, and I will show you how to fish for people!"

What a strange thing to say. What did he mean by "fishing for people"? Keep in mind, they didn't know who Jesus was. But there must've been something in the way he said those commanding words that changed everything for Simon and Andrew. Immediately, they dropped their nets, jumped into the sea, swam to shore, and followed Jesus. No questions asked.

The three walked together up the shore. That's when Jesus spied my brother James and me in our father Zebedee's fishing boat as we repaired our broken nets. Jesus called us to follow him too. And without hesitation, we left our father behind and began the adventure of following the Light of the World.

John Reflects

From that moment forward, Jesus continued his walking journeys all around the Sea of Galilee—and we followed him. Whenever he found a synagogue (a Jewish church), he would teach the people on Saturdays. **There he shared about his new Kingdom—not the flashy kingdoms of the world that Satan had shown him, but his Kingdom of light.** To prove that this new Kingdom was real, he healed all sorts of diseases and illnesses. Jesus became so popular that people would bring him all their sick loved ones to heal, and he healed them all.

Some were paralyzed (they couldn't walk). Some had epileptic seizures. Some were haunted by demons. Wherever we walked, people streamed behind us because they wanted to be healed, and they liked the idea of this new Kingdom of light and healing and freedom.

THE LIGHT MOMENT

Jesus experienced more temptation than we could ever imagine, yet in this sin-shadowed world, he shone brightly. He came to start a new Kingdom—not a flashy kingdom of the world, but a Kingdom of light—and he was calling people to join him there.

Questions for Conversation

What do you think it would have been like to be so hungry after forty days of no food? How did Jesus respond to Satan in the wilderness?

How do you think Satan's dark kingdom would be different from Jesus' Kingdom of light?

Prayer

Jesus, you are the Light of the World. I'm so grateful for you. Thank you for beating Satan in the wilderness. And thank you for calling me. Help me to follow you today. Amen.

JESUS TURNS WATER INTO WINE

God Can Do Anything!

(JOHN 2:1-11; 3:1-17)

How can you tell if it has rained outside? You might see a puddle and jump in it. *Splash!* Or you might hear water droplets fall off the leaves of plants. *Drip, drip, drip!* Or your nose might smell wet dirt. *Sniff!* We call these *signs*—things we notice in the world to prove something is true. We know all the signs of a rainy day. But guess what? I got to see seven special signs when Jesus was here. These signs showed me—and all of us—who Jesus is: God's Light in the world. In my book, the Gospel of John, I recorded these seven special signs, and I want to tell you about them, one by one.

A HUGE PROBLEM

After Jesus called me and the rest of the disciples to follow him, we went to a wedding. Have you been to a wedding before? They're really fun! Where I'm from, weddings last a long time—for days and days. We eat and laugh and dance and play. Jesus and all of us disciples were there, and Jesus' mom, Mary, came too. We all celebrated together, and everyone had plenty to eat and drink.

But then, uh oh! The hosts ran out of wine. That might seem silly or not very important, but it was actually a huge problem. Imagine having all your friends over for a party. You play games and have a lot of fun, but then you find out you don't have enough food for everyone. Someone will have a hungry tummy. And then you see there's nothing to drink at all. No juice or water or anything. Everyone will be thirsty. That's not a good party at all. How would you feel? It's embarrassing, isn't it?

That's how the wedding hosts felt. If they had no wine, the party would stop early—so stressful! People would talk, maybe even get mad. Then the family would always be known for not taking care of their guests.

JESUS CAN HELP

Mary noticed the problem, and she had a brilliant idea. Jesus could help. He could do anything because he's God. He could bring wine to this wedding and save the family from being embarrassed. She believed it with all her heart. So she grabbed his hand and pulled him aside. "They have no more wine," she said.

"Dear woman, that's not our problem," Jesus replied. "My time has not yet come."

Why do you think Jesus answered his mom that way? Was he being mean? No way! Jesus was never mean. So why did he say his time hadn't come yet?

You see, Jesus followed his Father, God, perfectly. His Father had a plan for how Jesus would live and then rescue the world. Jesus knew the plan, which means he knew how people would react once he started doing miracles. Big crowds would gather around him, and they'd want him to do more and more amazing things. It wasn't the right time just yet to announce who he was to the world.

But he also loved his mom. She wanted him to help, so he would. He would always obey God's commandment to honor your mom and dad, not just because he loved his heavenly Father, but because he loved his mom too. He could obey her wishes while making sure only a few people knew about his power.

Mary turned to the servants and told them, "Do whatever he tells you."

THE FIRST SIGN

Jesus spotted six large jars nearby. The jars were so big that you could probably hide inside them. He spoke to the servants, saying, "Fill these up to the tippy-top with water." So they did.

Jesus checked each one and said, "Go give these to the man in charge of the party."

The servants thought Jesus had made a mistake. They didn't need water—they needed wine. But they did what he asked, even though they felt silly.

When the man in charge looked inside the jugs, guess what he found? Bright red wine! He took a taste, and his eyes widened. "Yum! Bring me the man who just got married."

The newly married man rushed over, nervous because he knew all the wine was gone. To his surprise, the man in charge had a full glass. He clapped the married man on the shoulder, "You're an amazing host! Most people share all the best wine first, but you've saved the best for last."

The married man and his family didn't know how it happened, but their family's reputation was saved. All of us disciples watched in amazement—Jesus could do anything! We'd witnessed our first sign that Jesus was the Rescuer, the Light of the World. And this sign showed that just like a wedding celebration, Jesus' Kingdom would be a place with plenty of good things for everyone to enjoy.

BORN AGAIN

Word started to get out about Jesus. An important leader named Nicodemus heard about how powerful Jesus was, and he had questions. Nervous about what people would think, he snuck over to see Jesus in the middle of the night.

Jesus said to him, "If you want to see God's Kingdom, you have to be born again."

Nicodemus shook his head in confusion. Jesus' words made no sense. Did Jesus say we have to be born again? Was it possible to go back into his mother's womb and be born a second time? Not at all! So what was Jesus talking about?

Jesus was speaking about what happens when someone decides to follow him. **If you belong to Jesus, something amazing happens inside you. God makes you a whole new person, and it's like you've started a whole new life, kind of like a newborn baby. You belong to his family, and you're a member of his Kingdom.**

Jesus explained all of this to Nicodemus, but he still didn't understand. "How are these things possible?" Nicodemus asked.

GOD'S RESCUE PLAN

Jesus reassured him, saying, "This is how God loved the world: He gave his one and only Son, so that everyone who believes in him will not perish but have eternal life. God sent his Son into the world not to judge the world, but to save the world through him."

It's God's plan! Do you see it? God loves us so much that he sent Jesus to save us. Jesus is our Rescuer who gives us eternal life. Isn't that good news? I wish I could say Nicodemus finally understood, but it would take him a while to grasp what Jesus was saying.

John Reflects

Can you count all the way to seven? That's how many signs about Jesus we're going to find in our stories about him. We saw the first of the seven signs about Jesus when he turned water into wine. Just like puddles and wet dirt show us that rain has fallen, these signs will show us who Jesus is. He can do anything. **He's powerful, and he came with a mission: to rescue us. He's the Light of the World.**

THE LIGHT MOMENT

If you belong to Jesus, God makes you a whole new person, and you belong to his family and Kingdom. His Kingdom is a place of good things—like the wine at the wedding feast! He came to rescue us, because he is the Light of the World.

Questions for Conversation

What did you think of Jesus' first sign of turning water into wine? What else do you think Jesus can do with his power?

Nicodemus learned we become brand new like newborn babies when we follow Jesus. Do you want to follow Jesus? Do you believe he's God's Son, the Light of the World, and our Rescuer?

Prayer

Jesus, you are powerful. You can do anything! Thank you for loving us, giving us your light, and coming to rescue us. Amen.

STORY TWENTY-ONE

JESUS HEALS HURTING PEOPLE

Jesus Is a Healer

(JOHN 4:46-54; 5:1-20)

One of the things I loved most about Jesus was his compassion to heal all the folks who came to him with pain and stress and worry. Every day I spent with him, I saw miracles, and I had the joy of watching someone change from sick to healthy in a second. What a powerful Healer Jesus was!

As I mentioned before, I talked about the seven signs Jesus did in my book, the Gospel of John. The first one was when he turned water into wine.

Now let's talk about signs two and three. In these stories, Jesus healed two very different people. Pay very close attention to the types of folks Jesus loves to heal as you follow along.

THE SICK BOY

Jesus was traveling throughout the region of Galilee, sharing his message about the Kingdom. He visited his hometown of Nazareth, but the people there didn't believe in him. He said that prophets were often not taken seriously in their hometowns, but other people in Galilee opened their arms to Jesus. They'd seen him perform miracles in Jerusalem, and they hoped he would continue to heal all the sick people in their region.

When Jesus was near Capernaum, a city of that region, an official there had an extremely sick son, so sick that he was almost dead. Like any father who deeply loves his boy, he was worried and frantic. When he heard that Jesus was near, he found him, then got on his knees and begged Jesus to please come to his house to heal his sick son.

Jesus looked at the father with compassion, but then he asked something that surprised me. "Will you never believe in me unless you see miraculous signs and wonders?" I got the sense he wasn't saying this to the father so much as to the watching crowd—like he felt sad that people seemed to only chase after him for healing.

But the father was so worried, he didn't answer Jesus' question. He blurted out, "Lord, please come now before my little boy dies."

Jesus looked into the father's teary eyes and sighed. "Go back home," he told the scared father. "Your son will live!"

The man nodded, like he believed the words of Jesus.

I later learned that as he was walking home, the father's servants told him his son was alive and healthy. After confirming the time of day the boy recovered, the father realized his son had started to get better at exactly the time Jesus had said, "Your son will live!" The official's entire family started believing in Jesus. The boy had been so close to death he'd been almost there—yet just a faraway word from Jesus had brought him back to life.

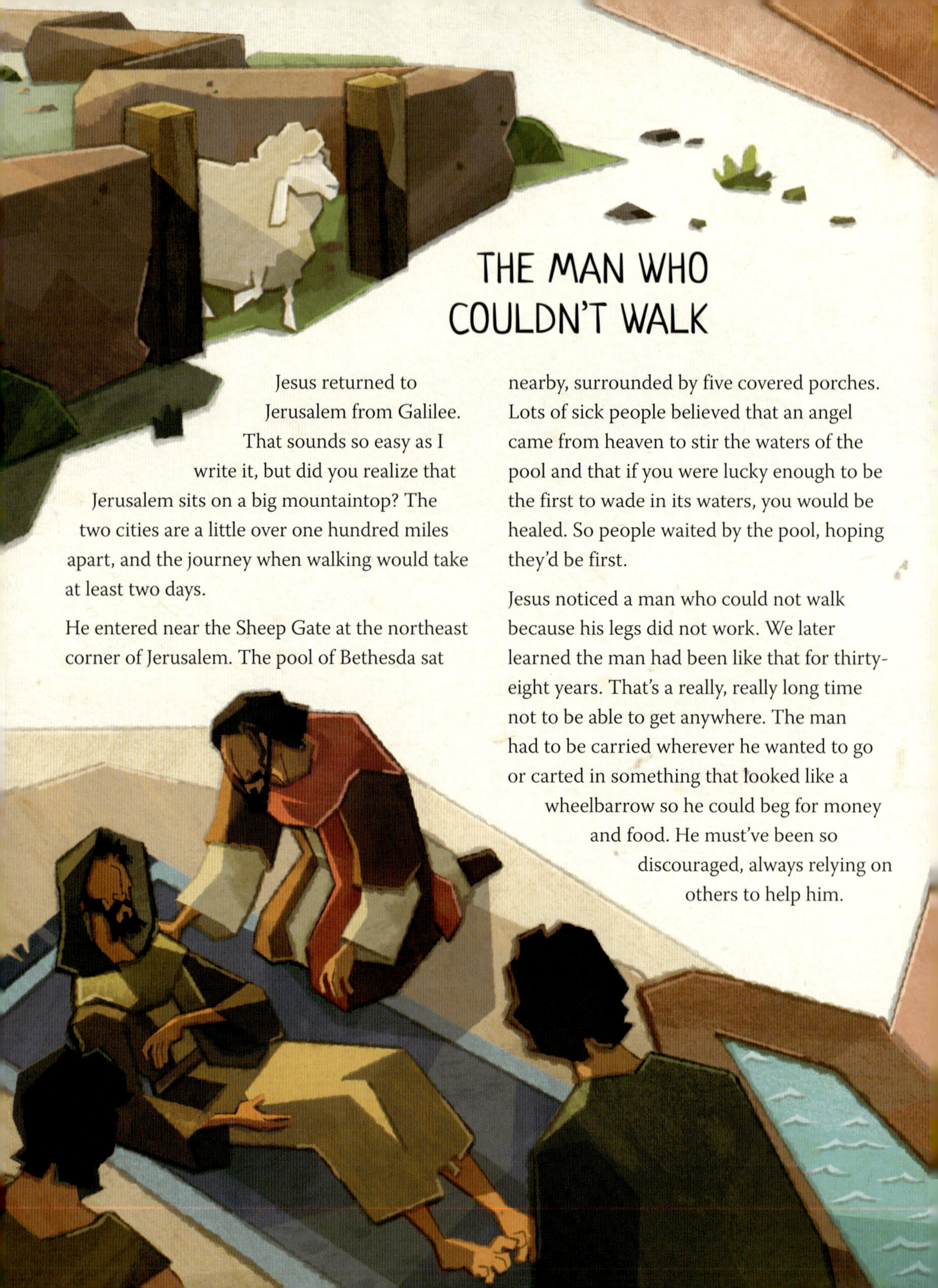

THE MAN WHO COULDN'T WALK

Jesus returned to Jerusalem from Galilee. That sounds so easy as I write it, but did you realize that Jerusalem sits on a big mountaintop? The two cities are a little over one hundred miles apart, and the journey when walking would take at least two days.

He entered near the Sheep Gate at the northeast corner of Jerusalem. The pool of Bethesda sat nearby, surrounded by five covered porches. Lots of sick people believed that an angel came from heaven to stir the waters of the pool and that if you were lucky enough to be the first to wade in its waters, you would be healed. So people waited by the pool, hoping they'd be first.

Jesus noticed a man who could not walk because his legs did not work. We later learned the man had been like that for thirty-eight years. That's a really, really long time not to be able to get anywhere. The man had to be carried wherever he wanted to go or carted in something that looked like a wheelbarrow so he could beg for money and food. He must've been so discouraged, always relying on others to help him.

WOULD YOU LIKE TO GET WELL?

Jesus asked him, "Would you like to get well?"

The man looked up at Jesus, who was surrounded by us, his disciples. I wonder if he was scared.

"I can't, sir," the sick man said, "for I have no one to put me in the pool when the water bubbles up. Someone else always gets there ahead of me."

In that moment, I realized the man never answered Jesus' question. I wonder why he gave another explanation. Maybe he was just so tired and sick. Maybe he had lost all hope.

Jesus came closer and bent low. "Stand up," he told the man. "Pick up your mat and walk!"

And do you know what happened next?

The man could feel his legs tingling and coming back to life. In a moment, he realized he could use them. He stood to his feet, an astonished look on his face. Laughing, he rolled up the mat he'd been resting on and then walked and walked and walked! Jesus changed ths man's life—when all seemed dark and impossible. His light broke through that darkness.

THE ANGRY LEADERS

This thirty-eight-year miracle in the making happened on the Sabbath, the day of rest for Jewish people. The religious leaders did not like that Jesus had dared to heal someone on their resting day. The leaders told the man, "You can't work on the Sabbath! The law doesn't allow you to carry that sleeping mat!"

The man shook his head. He couldn't believe the religious leaders were mad at him. After all, he had been unable to walk for thirty-eight years, and now he was healed! He told the leaders, "The man who healed me told me, 'Pick up your mat and walk.'"

"Who said such a thing as that?" they barked.

Jesus had already left, so the man had no idea who he was.

CONVERSATIONS

Later, Jesus visited the Temple and found the man he had healed. He looked at the man gently, with understanding and kindness. "Now you are well," he told the man. "So stop sinning, or something even worse may happen to you."

The man agreed. Then he went and told the religious leaders it had been Jesus who healed him.

This angered the leaders. They harassed Jesus because they believed he had broken the Sabbath rules.

Jesus answered their complaints by saying, "My Father is always working, and so am I."

This made them even angrier because when he called God "Father," he basically said he was equal with God.

Jesus continued, "The Father loves the Son and shows him everything he is doing. In fact, the Father will show him how to do even greater works than healing this man. Then you will truly be astonished."

The religious leaders had nothing to say back to Jesus. **If only they could have let his light in, like the people Jesus had healed! Even so, Jesus would continue to do miraculous healings, even on the Sabbath, bringing so much light to such dark places.**

John Reflects

Did you notice who Jesus loved to heal? It was the people who were broken, hurting, or oppressed. I never grew tired of watching him work. He would take a moment with each person, sometimes listening to their stories and giving them hope. Very often, Jesus would escape to the hillsides in the country to meet with his Father, asking him what he was to do next. I'm not sure when Jesus slept!

But he told me and the other disciples, "I tell you the truth, the Son can do nothing by himself. He does only what he sees the Father doing. Whatever the Father does, the Son also does." This reminds me how important it is for me to spend time with God so that his light reveals my heart and I know what to do. Did you know you can do that as well? You don't need a hillside or a wilderness, just a quiet place to listen.

THE LIGHT MOMENT

The light of Jesus was breaking into many people's lives: a worried bridegroom, an important official, a tired lame man. If only the religious leaders could have let his light in! Even so, Jesus would continue to heal many, bringing so much light to such dark places.

Questions for Conversation

Remember how God created the world with just his words? In this story, Jesus healed a sick boy with just his words. How does this help you see that Jesus is God's Son?

Why do you think the religious leaders were so mad that Jesus had healed someone on the Sabbath? What did they miss in their anger? How did their anger show they were walking in darkness?

Prayer

Jesus, thank you that you love to heal people. I want to lift up my friend or family member who needs your healing word or touch today. Would you please bring your light to them and heal them? Amen.

STORY TWENTY-TWO

JESUS FEEDS A CROWD AND WATER-WALKS

Jesus Takes Care of Us

(JOHN 6:1-21, 35)

Who takes care of you? Your mom and dad, your siblings, your grandparents, a teacher, or a friend? My parents and my brother, James, look after me. They make sure I have enough food to eat, they give me a warm bed to sleep in, and they always keep me safe. God provides kind, loving people in our lives to take care of us, but **Jesus also takes care of us.** That's what the next two signs (signs four and five) in our story show—just how much he cares about us.

THE HUNGRY CROWD

Jesus became pretty famous for all the amazing miracles he performed. People heard all about how he healed the sick and helped a man walk again. They wanted to see it for themselves. So wherever we went, large crowds came too. We couldn't get away from them. Hundreds, sometimes thousands, of people journeyed to see Jesus.

Jesus took us up a tall hill so we could get away from the crowds one day. Even though we tried our best, a group still found us. Soon enough, over five thousand people sat around, listening to Jesus teach and watching him perform miracles.

The hours ticked by, and our stomachs started to grumble. Have you ever heard your belly make a noise? We were hungry, and so were the thousands in the crowds.

And you know what? Jesus was hungry too. His stomach growled sometimes, too, just like mine and yours. That means he knows exactly how it feels when we need to eat. He noticed the restless crowd and felt the gurgle in his tummy, so he turned to Philip (one of the disciples), and said, “Where can we buy bread to feed all these people?”

Philip replied, “Even if we worked for months, we wouldn’t have enough money to feed them!”

Philip was right—we’d all have to work and work and work to make enough money to feed a giant crowd of people. It seemed impossible!

FOOD FOR EVERYONE

But then, Andrew (another disciple) brought a young boy to Jesus who had five loaves of bread and two fish. "This boy has a little bit of food," he said, "but that's nothing to five thousand people."

Jesus smiled. He knew what to do. "Tell everyone to sit down and get ready to eat," he said to the disciples.

We all felt a little silly, telling people to prepare for a meal in that moment. Even if everyone got one tiny crumb, there wouldn't be enough for everyone. But we also trusted Jesus. He could heal people, so maybe he could take care of these people's hunger too.

Taking the loaves of bread, Jesus broke them and gave thanks to God. He passed me a piece, and I broke it and passed it to Andrew.

When you split a piece of bread with someone, it gets smaller, right? That's how it's supposed to be. You break bread to share it, but you and your friend each get a half, not a whole piece.

Well, as the disciples and I took pieces of bread and passed them, the bread never ran out. It kept multiplying over and over again until every single person had enough bread to eat. Jesus made the impossible possible!

Jesus did the same thing with the fish. More and more fish appeared, and we never ran out. Each person ate until their stomachs stuck out a little bit because they were so full. I patted mine, satisfied with the dinner.

Jesus provided the perfect meal. He took care of all of us.

When everyone finished eating, Jesus gathered me and the other disciples together. "Now gather the leftovers, so that nothing is wasted."

We ran around to each person, picking up all the leftover food. When we were done, we had twelve whole baskets full of fish and bread. **Jesus didn't just give us *some* food; he gave us more than enough.**

THE BREAD OF LIFE

The people in the crowd loved the miracle Jesus performed. They cheered with joy and wondered how they could make Jesus their king—a king who could feed them. But you and I know that Jesus was already the King and his job wasn't just to feed people. He came to rescue us.

He couldn't be the kind of king they wanted—a ruler who would feed them and destroy their enemies. No, Jesus is the kind of king who rescues us from sin and death. And he feeds us in a lot of ways, but most importantly with his truth. When we hear and believe Jesus' words, it's like taking a big bite of yummy food. Our minds and hearts fill up with God's good truth, just like a belly full of food.

Jesus explained it like this: "I am the Bread of Life. Whoever comes to me will never be hungry again. Whoever believes in me will never be thirsty." Believing in Jesus is like eating one meal and never being hungry ever again. The thousands on the hill didn't get it. They just wanted him to give them actual food all the time.

Jesus knew what the crowd thought, so he slipped away to be by himself.

THE WATER ROAD

The other disciples and I waited for him. We climbed down the hill and prepared our boat to cross over the lake. As the sun set, we looked for Jesus, but he was nowhere to be found. So we decided to set sail without him. *Maybe he already crossed in another boat,* we thought.

As we reached the middle of the lake, the wind picked up. Then the clouds rumbled and burst, pouring rain onto us. The boat rocked back and forth. The waves splashed so high that water got into the boat. My heart pounded. Our boat could flip over, and we would all drown. What were we going to do?

Just then, I spotted someone walking on the water. What? How could someone stand on top of the water without falling in? Could it be a ghost? All of us shouted, terrified of what could be approaching our boat in the middle of the storm.

Then we heard a familiar voice calling out over the wind and the waves, saying, "Don't be afraid. I am here!"

It was Jesus!

Of course it was him. Who else could possibly be powerful enough to treat the water as a road? We paddled faster and faster to get to him. When he climbed into the boat with us, the storm stopped, and somehow our boat hit the shore.

We made it across the lake, safe and sound. Jesus took the very best care of us. He made sure the storm didn't hurt us, he comforted us, and he brought us to the shore.

John Reflects

As the Light of the World, Jesus takes care of us because he loves us. If Jesus can feed over five thousand people with five loaves and two fish, he can provide for you. And if Jesus can walk on choppy, stormy waters to save his friends, he can help you when you feel scared. His light can shine in any situation.

THE LIGHT MOMENT

Jesus provides for our needs—giving not just a little bit, but more than enough. When we're frightened, he's there to calm the storms. He's the Light of the World, and he takes care of us because he loves us.

Questions for Conversation

Which miracle—feeding the crowd or walking on water—do you wish you could have seen in person? How does the miracle show how much Jesus cares about us?

When has Jesus taken care of you, shining his light in a space where you felt needy or scared? Take a moment to thank him for being kind to you.

Prayer

Jesus, thank you that you can take care of me no matter what, and shine your light into my darkest moments. Could you help me with my problems today? I trust you can. Amen.

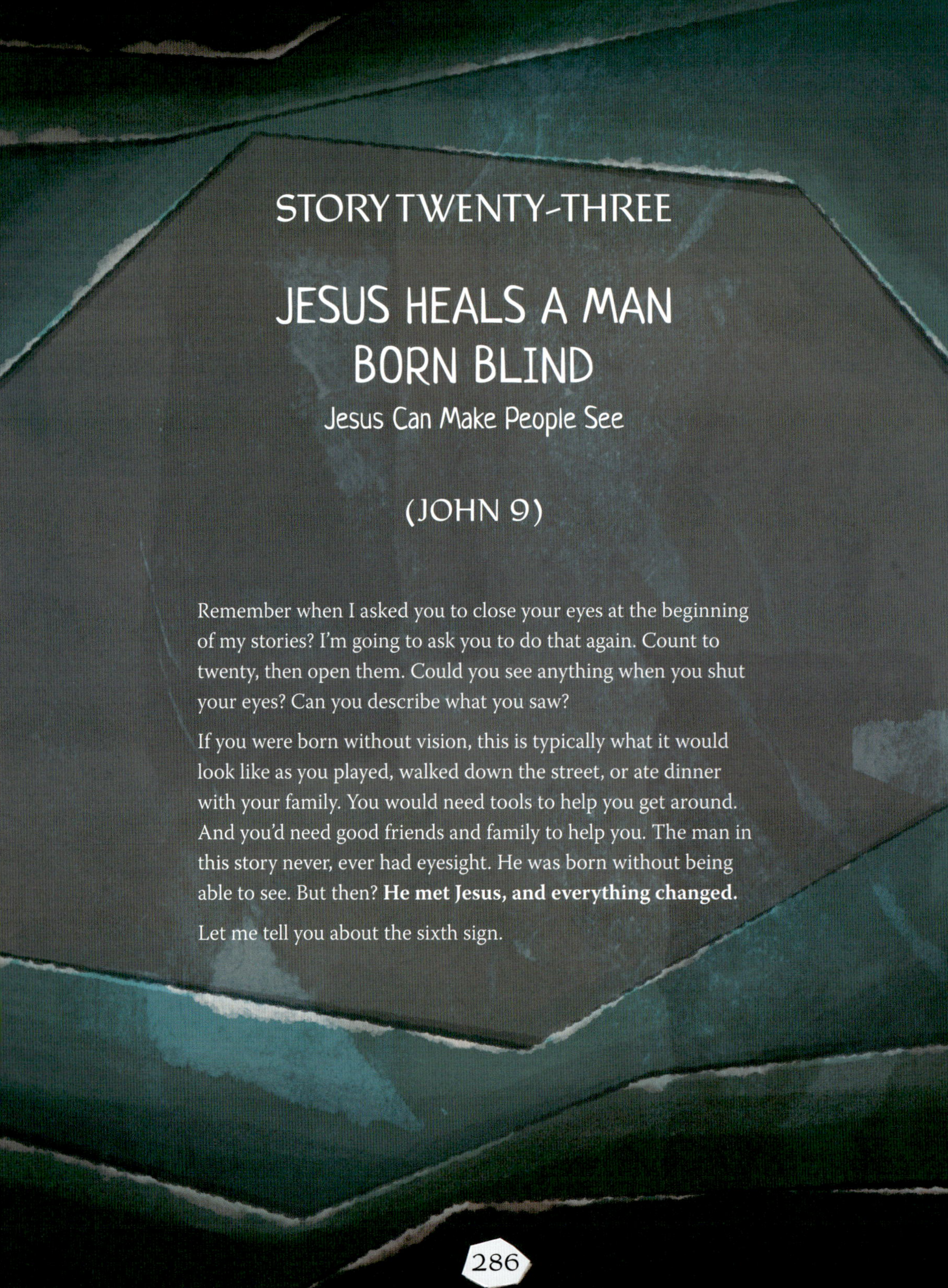

STORY TWENTY-THREE

JESUS HEALS A MAN BORN BLIND

Jesus Can Make People See

(JOHN 9)

Remember when I asked you to close your eyes at the beginning of my stories? I'm going to ask you to do that again. Count to twenty, then open them. Could you see anything when you shut your eyes? Can you describe what you saw?

If you were born without vision, this is typically what it would look like as you played, walked down the street, or ate dinner with your family. You would need tools to help you get around. And you'd need good friends and family to help you. The man in this story never, ever had eyesight. He was born without being able to see. But then? **He met Jesus, and everything changed.**

Let me tell you about the sixth sign.

A STRANGE QUESTION

As Jesus toured the countryside with us, his disciples, we met a man born blind who was begging by the roadside.

"Rabbi," we asked Jesus, "why was this man born blind? Was it because of his own sins or his parents' sins?" I had been taught that if you had an illness or a condition, it must be because someone had sinned, and I wanted to know how this blindness had come to be.

Jesus shook his head. "It was not because of his sins or his parents' sins."

For a moment, Jesus simply looked at me, compassion in his eyes. His words made no sense. There had to be a reason for this man's blindness.

"This happened," Jesus said, "so that God's power will be seen in him. We must quickly do what God sent us to do."

My heart jumped when Jesus said this. Jesus told us once that he only did what he saw his Father doing. Did God tell him to heal this man?

Jesus looked toward the darkening skyline. "The night is coming, and then no one can work. But while I am here in the world, I am the Light of the World."

There were those words again. The Light of the World. But could he do the impossible? No one had ever seen a person born blind regain his sight.

SPIT MUD

I watched as Jesus spit onto the dusty earth. Quickly, he made mud from his spit and the dirt, making a dull brown paste. In the next moment, he called the blind man toward him, then put the spit-mud all over his eyes. Can you imagine what the blind man was thinking when Jesus did that?

"Go wash in the pool of Siloam," Jesus told the man.

The man obeyed Jesus and washed in the pool. The moment water touched his muddied eyes, he could see! He leapt and danced and marveled at the trees, the grass, the sky, and people's faces. What a beautiful world he could see!

CONFUSION

All at once, the man started telling everyone he knew in the village that he had been healed of his blindness. "I can see!" he sang.

But some of his neighbors who had known him his whole life were too astonished to believe it. One said, "Isn't this the man who used to sit and beg?"

Some townspeople said yes, he was that man.

But, oddly, others said, "No, he just looks like him!"

The man who had been blind kept shouting, "Yes, I am the same one!"

Another villager asked him, "Who healed you? What happened?"

"The man they call Jesus made mud and spread it over my eyes and told me, 'Go to the pool of Siloam and wash yourself.' So I went and washed, and now I can see!"

Another asked, "Where is he now?"

But the man didn't know where Jesus had journeyed.

IN TROUBLE?

Instead of throwing a "He Can See" party, the leaders of the town took the man to the local Pharisees because this miraculous healing had happened on the Sabbath. (Sound familiar?)

In the local synagogue, the Pharisees asked him about the healing.

The man replied, "He put the mud over my eyes, and when I washed it away, I could see!"

This started a big argument between different Pharisees. One shouted, "This man Jesus is not from God, for he is working on the Sabbath."

Another hollered back, "But how could an ordinary sinner do such miraculous signs?"

The man stepped back. This was getting uncomfortable. All he really wanted to do was walk everywhere unassisted and see God's beautiful creation.

Finally, one of the Pharisees asked, "What's your opinion about this man who healed you?"

"I think he must be a prophet," he told the group of angry men.

THE BLIND MAN'S PARENTS

The Pharisees did not want to believe the blind-now-seeing man's story, so they made his parents come speak with them. They asked if this was their son and whether or not he was born blind—and if he was, how was it that he could now see perfectly.

His father was afraid of the Pharisees because they had a lot of power. No one wanted to cross them, and there was a rumor that if anyone gave Jesus credit for miracles, they'd be thrown out of the synagogue. He said, "We know that this is our son and that he was born blind, but we don't know how he can see or who healed him. Ask him. He is old enough to speak for himself."

ASKING AGAIN

The Pharisees didn't like the parents' answers, so they brought in the man born blind again. One said, "God should get the glory for this, because we know this man Jesus is a sinner."

The now-seeing man smiled, then laughed. "I don't know whether he is a sinner," he said. "But I know this: I was blind, and now I can see!"

"But what did he do?" they asked. "How did he heal you?"

The man grew tired of all this questioning. He shook his head. Why couldn't these leaders just leave him be? "Look," he finally said. "I told you once. Didn't you listen? Why do you want to hear it again? Do you want to become his disciples, too?"

Their faces reddened. They obviously did not like Jesus. They said, "We don't even know where this man comes from."

By now, the man had had enough. He was no longer afraid of the Pharisees. "Why, that's very strange! He healed my eyes, and yet you don't know where he comes from?" He looked into each face of the men bothering him. "We know that God doesn't listen to sinners, but he is ready to hear those who worship him and do his will."

The man continued. "Ever since the world began, no one has been able to open the eyes of someone born blind. If this man were not from God, he couldn't have done it."

By now, all the Pharisees were shouting and yelling and hollering, faces red. One said, "You were born a total sinner! Are you trying to teach us?" With that question, they grabbed him by his tunic and threw him out of the synagogue.

He walked away, a smile on his face as he noticed the leaves on the trees, the smiles on children's faces, and the bluest of blue skies.

John Reflects

It was later that Jesus pulled this man aside. I watched as Jesus asked him, “Do you believe in the Son of Man?”

The no-longer-blind man asked, “Who is he, sir? I want to believe in him.”

“You have seen him,” Jesus said with a smile, “and he is speaking to you.”

“Yes, Lord, I believe!” The man bowed to the ground, kissing the dust that Jesus had previously spit on. He worshiped Jesus, who had changed his entire world.

Every day we have the chance to worship Jesus. **We once were blind (we didn’t know Jesus), but now we see he is the one who saved the world from sin.** We have the joy of spending the rest of our lives worshiping the God who gives sight to the blind and brings light to this dark world.

THE LIGHT MOMENT

When the man born blind met Jesus, everything changed. Jesus, the Light of the World, gave him back his sight. We, too, were once blind, but now we see that he is the one who saved the world from sin.

Questions for Conversation

Why do you think the man was frustrated with the Pharisees? Would you have been?

What must it have been like not to see, then suddenly be able to see? Why do you think the man allowed Jesus to put spit-mud on his eyes, and why do you think he obeyed Jesus' command to wash in the pool?

Prayer

Jesus, I am grateful for you. Thank you for doing such powerful miracles like this one. You truly are the Light of the World. Amen.

STORY TWENTY-FOUR

JESUS RAISES A DEAD MAN TO LIFE

Jesus Gives Us Life

(JOHN 11:1-45)

Have you felt sad before? When I'm sad, tears fall down my face, and my heart feels heavy. I wonder what sadness feels like for you. The truth is, all of us have been sad and will be sad again. It's a part of life. That means Jesus also felt sadness. He cried, and his heart weighed him down. He knows what it's like to be sad.

In this story, we'll discover our last sign about Jesus, the Light of the World. It starts off sad, but it ends in the happiest way. And this story will show us one of the most important things about Jesus: He gives us life.

This is the seventh sign Jesus performed, and it was the most unbelievable of all!

A SAD MESSAGE

I was with Jesus and the other disciples when a messenger rushed over to Jesus. We all leaned in to hear what he had to say. The messenger caught his breath and said, "Lord, your dear friend is very sick."

"Who?" I asked. Jesus had many friends.

Jesus nodded, "Lazarus. I know he's very sick."

I knew Lazarus too. He had two sisters named Mary and Martha, who would always take care of us when we were in their town. Jesus loved them very much. All of us did. So I started packing my bag—we had to go help Lazarus.

"Are we leaving right away?" I asked Jesus. "We have to get there before anything worse happens to Lazarus."

Jesus put a hand on my shoulder. "Lazarus's sickness will not end in death. No, it happened for the glory of God so that the Son of God will receive glory from this."

I believed Jesus, so when he said we'd stay put for two more days, I didn't question him. He always knew the right thing to do. He said Lazarus wouldn't die, so he would be okay when we went to see him.

IS LAZARUS ASLEEP?

Finally, two days later, Jesus announced, "Our friend Lazarus has fallen asleep, but now I will go and wake him up."

The other disciples and I thought that was a funny thing to say. If Lazarus slept, that meant he was okay. Anyone could wake him up from a nap. "Lord, if he is sleeping, he will soon get better," we replied.

Jesus shook his head. "Lazarus is dead. And for your sakes, I'm glad I wasn't there, for now you will really believe. Come, let's go see him."

I couldn't believe it! Jesus had said Lazarus wouldn't die. How could this happen? Jesus loved Lazarus. Why would he let something bad happen to him?

I had many questions, but no answers. Even so, I trusted Jesus. I had faith in him. So I followed him to Mary and Martha's house.

TO MARTHA AND MARY'S HOUSE

Many people crowded in the courtyard and alleyways around the sisters' home. They had come to grieve with the two women. Do you know what grieving is? It's when you feel very, very sad about something for a long time. It's not like when you cry because you stubbed your toe. It's more like how if you broke your arm, you're sad for a long time because you can't play with your friends until your arm gets better. Death makes us grieve—when someone dies, we're sad for a long time.

When Mary and Martha heard Jesus had arrived, Martha hurried to go see him, but Mary stayed inside. Martha came to Jesus, her face all puffy from crying so much. She said, "Jesus, if you had been here, Lazarus would still be alive. But I know God will give you whatever you ask."

Was Martha right? Could Jesus have healed Lazarus? Of course! He can heal anyone. But he didn't this time. Why? Well, Martha was about to find out.

Jesus told her, "Your brother will rise again."

Martha was confused. What could Jesus mean? Maybe he was talking about the future when we would all live with God forever, not now.

THE RESURRECTION

Jesus kept talking. "I am the Resurrection and the Life. Anyone who believes in me will live, even after dying. Everyone who lives in me and believes in me will never ever die. Do you believe this, Martha?"

"I do," she said. "I believe you are the Rescuer. You're God's Son, the Light of the World, here to save us all." Martha didn't understand what Jesus would do, but she had faith. She went to her sister, Mary, and told her Jesus wanted to see her. They went together to Lazarus's tomb, and the people at their house followed. Jesus was there, along with all of us disciples.

Mary fell down at Jesus' feet, crying. "Jesus, if you had been here, Lazarus wouldn't have died."

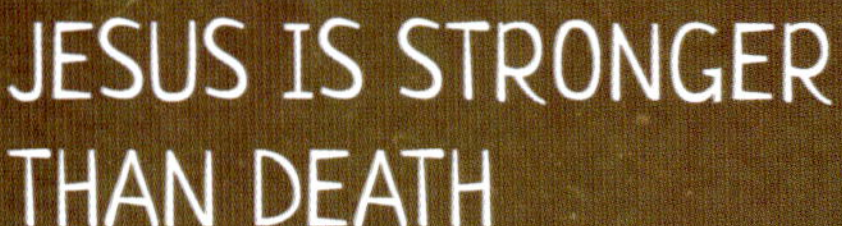

JESUS IS STRONGER THAN DEATH

Then something interesting happened. Jesus got angry! At Mary? No. He was angry at death. Remember back in the garden when Adam and Eve ate the forbidden fruit? When they sinned, death entered the world. Jesus hated that death had power over the people he loved. **So he came to destroy sin, death, and the sneaky snake, Satan, forever.** He was angry that death took his friend Lazarus, and he was going to do something about it.

"Where have you put him?" he asked the sisters.

They pointed to Lazarus's tomb, which was a place where we would put people who had died. It was like a small cave with a big stone rolled in front of it. Jesus cried and cried when he looked at the tomb. He cried for his friend, for Mary and Martha, and for all who had ever felt sad because of death.

He wiped his tears away and said, "Roll the stone away."

Martha gasped. "Jesus, if we do that, it will smell so bad! He's been dead for four whole days."

Jesus answered, "Didn't I tell you that you would see God's glory if you believe? Roll the stone away."

Some strong men gathered on one side of the huge stone and pushed, pushed, pushed. The stone creaked, then rolled aside. Light flooded into the tomb.

Jesus yelled, "Lazarus, come out!"

At first, nothing happened. The crowd hushed. Then we heard someone inside the tomb take a breath, then some steps. Sure enough, there was Lazarus, wrapped in graveclothes but walking and talking. He was alive! **When Jesus called, the darkness of death could not keep Lazarus down.**

John Reflects

Many people believed in Jesus after they saw Lazarus come out of that grave. It was the greatest sign of all because it showed us that Jesus gives us life. He is stronger than death. That's why he told Martha that he was the Resurrection and the Life. If we believe in him, we will live with him forever and ever.

THE LIGHT MOMENT

The seventh sign Jesus performed was the most unbelievable of all—he raised Lazarus from the dead! Jesus is the Resurrection and the Life, and he came to destroy sin and death forever. The darkness of death could not keep Lazarus in the tomb.

Questions for Conversation

When have you felt sad?
When you were sad, do you think Jesus was sad too?
How would you have felt seeing Lazarus come out of the grave?
Do you believe Jesus gives you life?

Prayer

Jesus, your light is stronger than death. You know what it's like to be sad, so can you help me when I feel sad? Thank you for giving me life. Amen.

STORY TWENTY-FIVE

JESUS DIED FOR OUR SINS

Jesus Sacrificed Everything to Save Us

(JOHN 13, 18–19)

Have you ever had to give bad news to someone? Did your stomach hurt before you told them? Did your palms sweat? Was your mouth dry? That's how I feel right now because this story is really hard to tell. I promise it doesn't end so sadly, but please bear with me.

I loved Jesus with everything inside me. And he loved me so much that when I wrote my book, I called myself "the disciple whom Jesus loved." There's a word for that: *beloved*. To be loved by Jesus is the best feeling in the world.

And I'm going to tell you just how much he loves you.

UPPER ROOM

We all met in a room at the top of a house to celebrate the Passover. Remember the story of the exodus, when Moses led the Israelites away from Pharaoh and through the Red Sea? Well, at the same time every year, Jewish people celebrate Passover with a meal where we reenact the last plague, the one where God passed over our houses and saved us.

During our celebration, Jesus did the unthinkable. He washed our feet. He told us the Passover bread was his body, and that the wine was his blood—something I would remember later. He loved us to the very end, but he also said that one of us would betray him. I worried it might be me. We all worried, actually. He prayed for us all, and he even prayed for you—for anyone who would one day believe in Jesus.

ARREST

We all went to a garden of olive trees. Then Jesus took me, James, and Peter aside, and he prayed and agonized. We kept falling asleep, which made me sad. Why couldn't I stay awake? But the length of the day and the darkness of night made my eyelids heavy.

But soon we were fully awake.

Roman soldiers and Temple guards with torches and lanterns raged into the garden. They carried weapons, and their faces looked angry, especially because of the flames. They didn't like that people said Jesus was the King. Their only king was Caesar! Who did this Jesus think he was anyway?

Jesus approached the scary crowd. "Who are you looking for?"

"Jesus the Nazarene," one soldier spit out, as if Jesus' name were ugly.

Judas stood right there. I knew then that he had been the one to betray Jesus.

To my right, Peter pulled out a sword, then cut off the ear of Malchus, the slave of the high priest. I was shocked, but Jesus quickly healed the man.

Jesus said, "Put your sword back into its sheath. Shall I not drink from the cup of suffering the Father has given me?"

THE HIGH PRIEST'S HOUSE

All at once, the soldiers and the guards arrested Jesus, like he was a criminal. They tied his hands and eventually took him to the house of the high priest, who questioned Jesus about what he'd been teaching people and who his followers were. They thought Jesus was going to ruin their lives and set up a new kingdom. They didn't understand that Jesus' Kingdom wasn't about toppling a government—it was about bringing light to the world.

Jesus reminded him that everyone knew what he taught because he spoke freely in public. “I have not spoken in secret. Why are you asking me this question? Ask those who heard me. They know what I said.”

One of the Temple guards smacked Jesus. “Is that the way to answer the high priest?” he barked.

“If I said anything wrong, you must prove it,” Jesus answered. “But if I am speaking the truth, why are you beating me?”

GOVERNOR PILATE

This back-and-forth trial at the high priest's house happened until the wee hours of the morning. In a rush, the Jewish leaders sent Jesus to Pilate, who governed Judea. They hoped Pilate would punish Jesus for talking about his new Kingdom of light, which their hearts weren't ready to believe in. None of the leaders stepped inside Pilate's palace because it would make them unclean. Pilate had to step outside to hear their charges against Jesus. "What is your charge against this man?" Pilate asked. He rubbed sleep from his eyes, as it was quite early that Friday morning.

One leader called out, "We wouldn't have handed him over to you if he weren't a criminal!"

But Pilate didn't want to be bothered with this. He told them to deal with Jesus using their own law. This wasn't his responsibility.

The Jewish leaders reminded Pilate that only Rome could kill a prisoner.

Pilate shook his head. Why did these mean men want to harm Jesus? He invited Jesus into his palace. "Are you the king of the Jews?" he asked.

"My Kingdom is not an earthly kingdom," Jesus replied. "If it were, my followers would fight to keep me from being handed over to the Jewish leaders."

"So you are a king?" Pilate asked. Throughout their conversation, Pilate had a hard time understanding what the Jews wanted him to do with Jesus. He didn't think Jesus was trying to lead a rebellion against Rome. So he devised a plan. Every year at Passover, he had a tradition to release one Jewish prisoner. He asked the leaders if they wanted him to choose Jesus.

But they didn't want Jesus to be set free. Instead they asked for a man named Barabbas, who was a hardened criminal. Pilate knew Jesus wasn't guilty of anything, but he was so afraid of the crowd gathering outside that he let them have their way.

CRUCIFY HIM!

Pilate ordered Jesus to be whipped. Some of his soldiers wove a crown from a thorny plant, then pressed it onto Jesus' head. They made fun of Jesus and yelled at him in a mocking tone. "Hail! King of the Jews!" They slapped Jesus too. Even though Pilate believed Jesus to be innocent, he pushed Jesus outside in front of the crowd. He stood there, bloody and hurting, before the people and the Jewish leaders.

"Look," Pilate shouted. "Here is the man!"

The chief priests and the Temple guards stirred the people into a frenzy. They shouted, "Crucify him! Crucify him!"

Pilate again said he didn't find any guilt in Jesus.

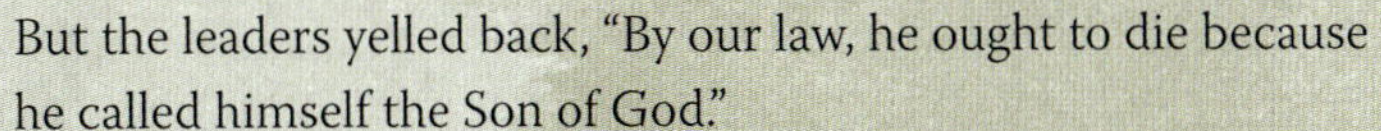

But the leaders yelled back, "By our law, he ought to die because he called himself the Son of God."

Pilate pulled Jesus back inside. He was terrified hearing this news. He asked Jesus where he came from. But Jesus would not answer him.

Finally, he pleaded, "Don't you realize that I have the power to release you or crucify you?"

Jesus spoke then. "You would have no power over me at all unless it were given to you from above. So the one who handed me over to you has the greater sin."

HIGH NOON

Desperate, Pilate tried to release Jesus. It was now noon, and the sun beat down on everyone, high in the sky.

But from below, in the courtyard, the Jewish leaders screamed, "If you release this man, you are no friend of Caesar. Anyone who declares himself a king is a rebel against Caesar."

Pilate was an official under Caesar, who led the entire Roman Empire from Rome—so Pilate had to always carry out the will of Caesar. Pilate brought Jesus back before the people. He went up on a high platform and sat in his judgment seat. "Look," he shouted, "here is your king!"

But instead of worshiping Jesus as their king, the leaders yelled, "Away with him! Crucify him!"

"What? Crucify your king?" Pilate asked.

"We have no king but Caesar," the priests replied.

THE CRUCIFIXION

The soldiers took Jesus away from Pilate's palace. They strapped Jesus' wrists to a heavy wooden beam so that his hands were wide apart, like he was hugging the whole, wide world. Underneath the weight of this heavy wood, he walked and stumbled to a place called Golgotha, where they planned to kill him.

At Golgotha, which means Place of the Skull, the Roman soldiers cruelly nailed Jesus to the cross. They fastened a sign to the top of Jesus' cross that read, "Jesus of Nazareth, the King of the Jews." Two notorious criminals were being crucified on either side of Jesus.

The soldiers took Jesus' clothes and played a betting game to see who would get his tunic.

A NEW FAMILY

That's when Jesus noticed me. I stood weeping next to his mother, Mary, as well as two other Marys, Mary Magdalene and Mary the wife of Clopas.

Jesus pulled in an agonizing breath. "Dear woman," he said to his mom, "here is your son."

He looked right at me, love emanating from his teary eyes. "Here is your mother," he choked.

Even in death, Jesus took care of me, loved me, provided for me. It was too much to bear. I hugged Mary, and she embraced me fiercely. We wept together.

JESUS DIED

Jesus gulped another bit of air. “I am thirsty,” he said.

Someone below the cross hoisted a sponge full of sour wine on a hyssop branch and held it to Jesus’ dried lips. Jesus tasted it.

That’s when Jesus said his last words. “It is finished.” His head bowed. His final breath released. **And the world grew dark.**

A soldier pierced Jesus’ side with a spear—blood and water poured out.

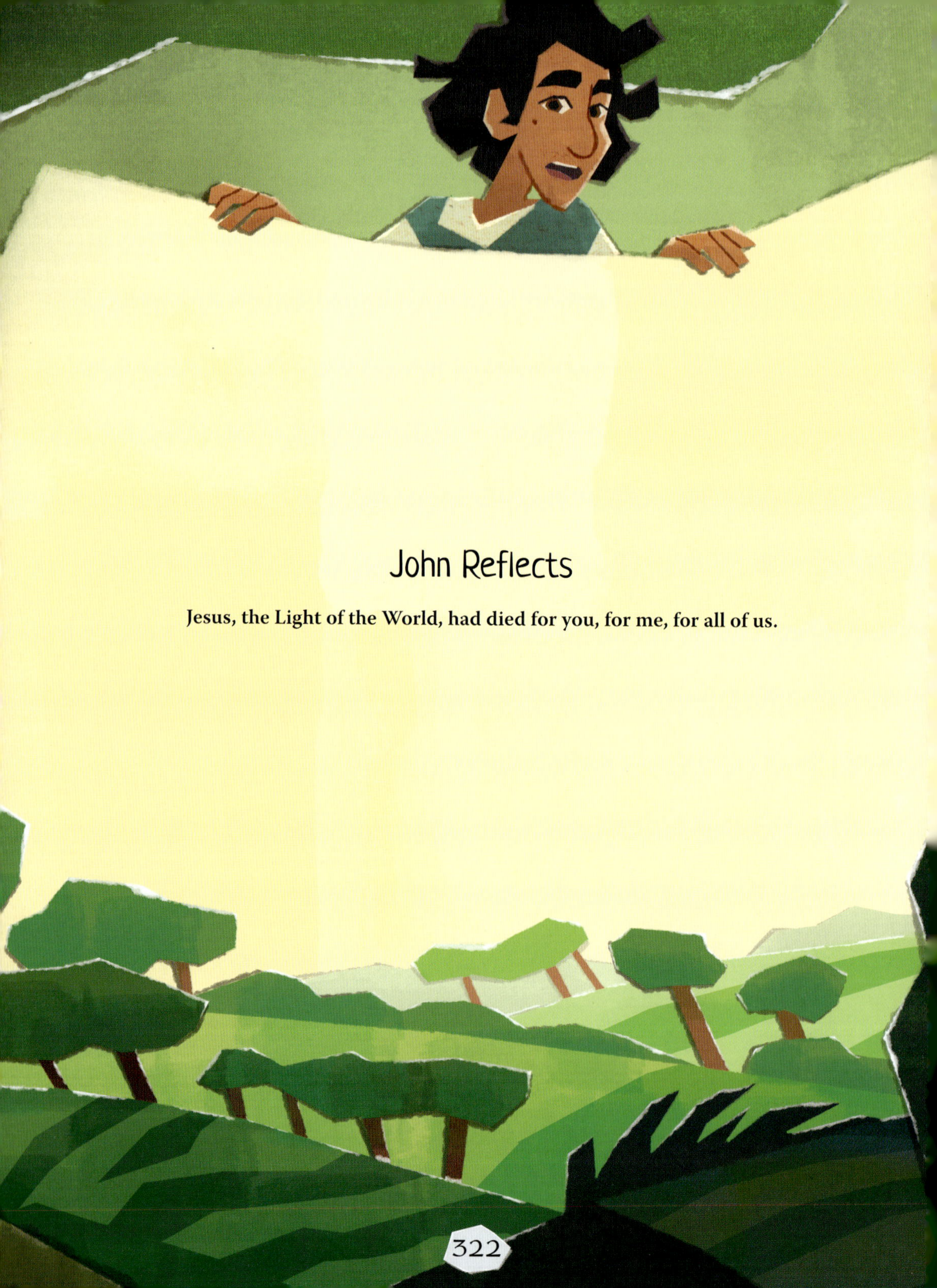

John Reflects

Jesus, the Light of the World, had died for you, for me, for all of us.

THE LIGHT MOMENT

To be loved by Jesus is the best feeling in the world, and in the crucifixion, he showed us his love like never before. At his death, the world grew dark. Jesus, the Light of the World, died for you, me, and all of us.

Questions for Conversation

Why do you think the Jewish leaders wanted to crucify Jesus and snuff out his life?

Why do you think the world suddenly grew dark the moment Jesus died?

Prayer

Jesus, thank you so much for going through all that mocking, beating, and pain for me. You endured the worst darkness! I don't know what to say. I'm grateful for how much you love me. Amen.

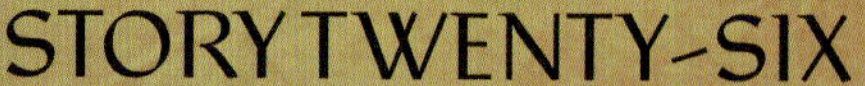

STORY TWENTY-SIX

JESUS IS ALIVE

Death Did Not Win

(LUKE 24:1-12; JOHN 20:1-23)

Have you ever been in a really dark room? When Jesus died, darkness fell over the earth. But for me and the other disciples, it felt like darkness covered everything inside of us too. Our hearts weighed us down, and all we wanted to do was cry.

But what does it feel like when you finally turn the light on in a dark place? It's the best feeling ever! **Being in God's family means you can always find the light, even when everything seems as black as the night.** And this story is why that's true for me and you.

JESUS IN THE TOMB

When Jesus died, a secret follower of Jesus named Joseph went to Pilate.

"Can I take the body of Jesus?" he asked.

"You may," replied Pilate.

Joseph needed help carrying Jesus' body, so Nicodemus (the man who had spoken to Jesus before about being born again) helped him. They wrapped up Jesus' body and placed him in a tomb, just like Mary and Martha did for Lazarus when he died. They rolled a giant stone in front of the entrance. No one could get in.

The disciples and I, along with the women who followed Jesus, stayed together the next day, which was Saturday. We cried and cried and tried to process what had happened to Jesus. But we couldn't. **None of it made sense.** Jesus was supposed to be the Light of the World, the Rescuer, the Son of God. Instead, he was dead in a tomb. Our world felt as dark as the night.

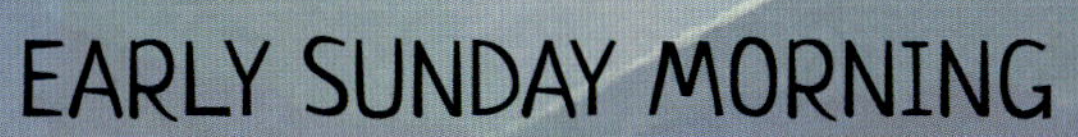

EARLY SUNDAY MORNING

Before the sun rose on Sunday morning, the women snuck away to take care of Jesus' body. But they didn't think about the large stone. How would they get inside the tomb? Maybe if they all worked together, they could roll the big rock away. Or maybe they could find someone to help. They would find a way.

They arrived at the tomb, which sat in a beautiful garden. As the sun peeked over the horizon, the birds began to sing. It would have been a happy morning if it weren't for the sadness of Jesus' death.

Looking around, the women noticed something strange. There was the tomb, but it wasn't sealed shut. The stone had been rolled away! What could this mean? They rushed inside the tomb and found it empty. Where was Jesus?

Maybe someone mean had taken Jesus' body away. They ran out, looking for a thief. Suddenly, two shining men appeared in front of them. They were angels, gleaming and smiling. The angels laughed and said to the women, "Why are you looking among the dead for someone who is alive? He isn't here! He is risen from the dead!"

GOOD NEWS

Could it be true? The women didn't know what to think, but they did know they had to tell someone what they had seen. They sprinted to where the other disciples and I stayed. Bursting through the door, they yelled, "The stone was rolled away! Come see for yourselves. The tomb is empty. Jesus is alive!"

Peter and I sprang up and ran with all our might, and Mary Magdalene followed. I got there first, but when I saw the open tomb, I couldn't move. Where was Jesus? Was this some terrible joke? Or could he actually be alive? Tears streamed down my face as Peter and Mary arrived.

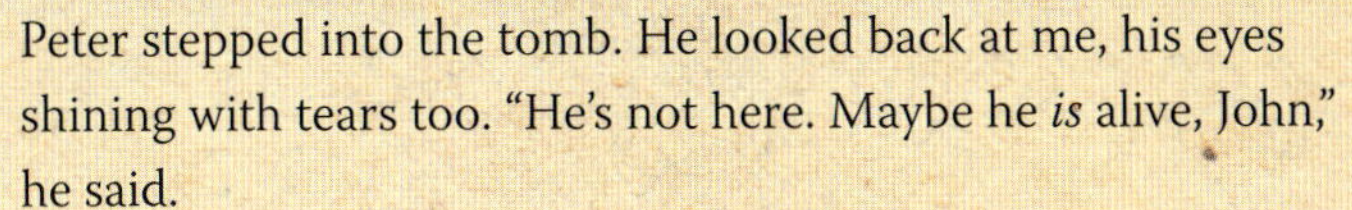

Peter stepped into the tomb. He looked back at me, his eyes shining with tears too. "He's not here. Maybe he *is* alive, John," he said.

Confused, we walked back to the others. We didn't know what to do or say or think. Would we see Jesus soon? Was the darkness over? Could he be alive?

“I HAVE SEEN THE LORD!”

Mary Magdalene stayed back at the tomb, weeping. She missed Jesus very much and didn’t understand where he had gone. She rose to leave and noticed a man standing nearby. He asked her, “Dear woman, why are you crying? Who are you looking for?”

She sniffed. “Sir, I am looking for Jesus. He died and was buried right over there. But he’s missing. If you know where he is, please tell me.”

Mary thought the man was the gardener—they were in a garden, after all. But guess who it actually was? It was Jesus! He called out her name, “Mary!”

When he said her name, she recognized it was Jesus. She ran up and hugged him, crying happy tears. "Teacher, you're alive," she exclaimed.

Jesus encouraged her, saying she should go tell the disciples she had seen him. So she did. She skipped all the way to find us, full of joy because Jesus was alive, not dead. Wearing the biggest smile, she said to us, "I have seen the Lord!" But some of us didn't believe her.

That evening, we kept hidden and locked the door. We were afraid that the mean people who killed Jesus might want to hurt us too. As we ate dinner, we chatted about Jesus. What did it all mean? Yesterday, we mourned the loss of our friend. But today, we had news of a miracle. Could it be true?

JESUS IS ALIVE

As we were eating, all of a sudden, Jesus stood among us! We all gasped. "Peace be with you," he said with a twinkle in his eye. He really was alive.

I hugged him tight, then the rest of the disciples took a turn. We could barely believe our eyes. We all knew he had died, yet there he was, laughing and hugging us all. He showed us the scars from the cross in his hands and side. He was Jesus, all right. My heart felt like it might burst from happiness. **The Light of the World had defeated darkness!**

John Reflects

In his death, Jesus shows us how much he loves us. In his resurrection, he displays that he is powerful, mighty, and King over everything. He's the one we were waiting for—our Rescuer who could save us from sin and death. Our Rescuer said to death, "No more!" The Light of the World, King Jesus, extinguished the darkness.

Since Jesus is alive, you and I have hope. His resurrection proves that one day, we will be resurrected too. Did you know that? Death isn't the end of the story for anyone who believes in Jesus. He has a happy future with him planned for us in his Kingdom. Do you know what to do so you can live there someday? Have faith. If you have faith in Jesus—if you believe he died to save you and is alive now as King—you are a part of God's family forever and ever.

THE LIGHT MOMENT

Being in God's family means you can always find the light, even when everything seems as black as the night. When Jesus died, none of it made sense. Until, three days later—Jesus appeared! The Light of the World had defeated darkness.

Questions for Conversation

How do you think John and the other disciples felt when they saw that Jesus was alive? How would you feel if you were there with them?

Do you believe Jesus is alive? Do you want to have faith in Jesus, who died for you and is alive today?

Prayer

Jesus, you are more powerful than death. Your light conquered the darkness, and you are alive! I have faith in you. Thank you for loving me so much. Amen.

STORY TWENTY-SEVEN

JESUS FLIES TO HEAVEN AND GIVES GIFTS

God Gave Us the Holy Spirit

(ACTS 1–2)

After Jesus came back to life, everything changed. He appeared to over five hundred people—full of life, vibrancy, and joy. He spent many days on the earth, teaching about the Kingdom of God and giving us instructions. The eleven remaining disciples often ate with him. And every time I saw him, I was so happy. I felt completely alive, like I knew who I was and what he had called me to do. I never wanted Jesus to leave us.

But let me tell you what happened next.

FORTY DAYS

Jesus stayed with us for forty days. You might think that's a long time, but we all sensed that our time with him was short. During one of our final meals together, Jesus looked at each of us with love in his eyes. He took a deep breath, then said, "Do not leave Jerusalem until the Father sends you the gift he promised, as I told you before." He held up a cup of water, then pointed to it. "John baptized with water, but in just a few days you will be baptized with the Holy Spirit."

I looked at Peter, confused. Peter shrugged. Neither of us knew what it meant to be baptized by something other than water. I tucked away Jesus' words, chewing on them as I went to sleep. How would the Holy Spirit baptize someone?

THE LAST DAY

Of course, I didn't know this would be Jesus' last day on the earth, but we all felt that he wouldn't be with us forever. So many questions bothered us, mostly about when Jesus was going to rid Jerusalem of Roman rule. It had been several weeks, and nothing had happened. Finally, I asked him straight up: "Lord, has the time come for you to free Israel and restore our kingdom?"

There on the Mount of Olives, Jesus looked right into my eyes. I noticed tears on his face. How many times had we misunderstood Jesus? I could see that I had asked the wrong question again. Jesus sighed. He gathered us around him. "The Father alone has the authority to set those dates and times, and they are not for you to know."

Even his correction was kind. My heart thumped wildly in my chest. What would he say next?

"But you will receive power when the Holy Spirit comes upon you."

I nudged Peter. Is this what Jesus meant about being baptized in the Holy Spirit?

Jesus continued, "**And you will be my witnesses, telling people about me everywhere**—in Jerusalem, throughout Judea, in Samaria, and to the ends of the earth."

Before I had a chance to react to this thrilling statement about our destinies, a cloud swept in from heaven. It hovered over the earth, white and puffy. I wondered what it meant.

Jesus, who once had his sandaled feet on the ground, was now hovering above the dust we stood on. Slowly, he rose toward the unusual cloud. It's hard for me to even describe it because I'm not quite sure what I was seeing. We all watched, hands shading our eyes from the sun, as Jesus ascended toward heaven until we could no longer see him.

THE VISITORS

Before we could react, I was startled to see two very tall men dressed in the brightest white robes. I shook in their presence.

"Men of Galilee," they said together, "why are you standing here staring into heaven?"

I wanted to answer back, "Because Jesus floated away," but I held my tongue.

"Jesus has been taken from you into heaven," they continued, "but someday he will return from heaven in the same way you saw him go."

Before we could respond, the two white-clothed men disappeared. We were left with no more explanation.

REPLACEMENT

We left the Mount of Olives and made our way to Jerusalem to an upper room in a home that many of us were staying in, as we tried to make sense of everything we had seen and heard. One hundred and twenty of us prayed, including Jesus' mother, Mary, many other women, and Jesus' brothers. Peter stood and shushed us. "We should replace Judas, who betrayed Jesus," he said.

The crowd put forward two men, Justus and Matthias, and Matthias was chosen to take Judas's place.

PENTECOST

Fifty days after Passover (when Jesus had his final meal with all of us) was Pentecost. Jesus had been in heaven for ten days now, and we kept gathering in the upper room, praying, praying, praying. We all wondered what would happen next as we sat and waited.

From above me, a roaring rush of wind blew through the room. I heard others gasp. In an instant, bright flames hovered over each of us, one tongue-like flame for every person in the upper room. This must be what Jesus meant when he talked about being baptized by the Holy Spirit. Suddenly, I felt warmed from the inside out. Joy erupted from inside me, and then I spoke and sang in a language I didn't recognize. And, let me tell you, it wasn't a whisper, but a shout!

I was so happy. Even though Jesus had returned to heaven, God's light was still with us.

We were all making such a commotion with different languages hollered between us that those in the courtyard below noticed; they ran toward our building. We met together on the street—us proclaiming words we could not understand, and people from all over the empire actually understanding everything we said! Afterward, we found people from all over the world—Parthians, Medes, Elamites, Mesopotamians, Judeans, Cappadocians, and folks from Pontus, Asia, Phrygia, Pamphylia, Egypt, Libya, Rome, Crete, and Arabia.

One woman said to me, "These people"—she pointed at us—"are all from Galilee, and yet we hear them speaking in our own native languages!" I nodded, not knowing what to say. But in the next moment, I couldn't stop smiling.

Another man said, "And we all hear these people speaking in our own languages about the wonderful things God has done!"

I looked at Peter. "What can this mean?"

But another person in the crowd snapped, "They're just drunk, that's all!"

PETER'S SERMON

Peter stood, no longer shrinking back in the safety of our upper room, but bold and confident. The Holy Spirit had certainly come upon him. He told the large gathering crowd that none of us were drunk—after all, it was only nine in the morning. He spoke of the prophet Joel, who had predicted this time in history.

Then he shared the story of Jesus. "God publicly endorsed Jesus the Nazarene by doing powerful miracles, wonders, and signs through him, as you well know."

I knew his words to be true. I had watched it all.

"But God knew what would happen, and his prearranged plan was carried out when Jesus was betrayed."

So all that pain and betrayal at the hands of Judas was a part of God's plan? I marveled at the thought. God could use even the evilest evil to carry out his plan.

"With the help of lawless Gentiles," Peter preached, "you nailed him to a cross and killed him."

That would be terrible indeed. Except . . .

"God released him from the horrors of death and raised him back to life, for death could not keep him in its grip."

The whole crowd gasped.

Then Peter summarized our last fifty days. "God raised Jesus from the dead, and we are all witnesses of this. Now he is exalted to the place of highest honor in heaven, at God's right hand. And the Father, as he had promised, gave him the Holy Spirit to pour out upon us, just as you see and hear today."

His words were beautifully true. I had witnessed it all.

Peter's words so affected the crowd that someone yelled out, "What should we do?"

Peter hushed the crowd. "Each of you must repent of your sins and turn to God, and be baptized in the name of Jesus Christ for the forgiveness of your sins. Then you will receive the gift of the Holy Spirit."

And wouldn't you know it? Three thousand people believed Peter's words and were baptized that day in Jerusalem.

John Reflects

Everything Jesus had said came true. He'd told us he would die for the people, and he had. He'd said he would bring light to this darkened world, and he had. He'd said he would be raised to life, and he had been. He'd promised he'd give us the Holy Spirit, and he did.

But I want to highlight another thing Peter said in his powerful sermon. "This promise is to you, to your children, and to those far away—all who have been called by the Lord our God." Did you catch that? Those words are for you. If you've been called by God to follow him, all these promises are for you too. When you meet Jesus, you also receive the promise of the Holy Spirit, a companion who will never ever leave you. What a gift!

THE LIGHT MOMENT

"Be my witnesses," Jesus said, before he returned to heaven. With a roaring rush of wind, the Holy Spirit came down on his followers in bright tongues of fire. Even though Jesus was gone, God's light still was with them.

Questions for Conversation

How would you feel if you saw Jesus float into a cloud into the bright sky?

What did Peter say we needed to do to be saved from the darkness of our sins?
Have you had that experience yet?

Prayer

Jesus, I choose to repent, turn away from my sins, and follow after you forever in the light. You are worth it. Please remind me that the Holy Spirit now lives inside me. Amen.

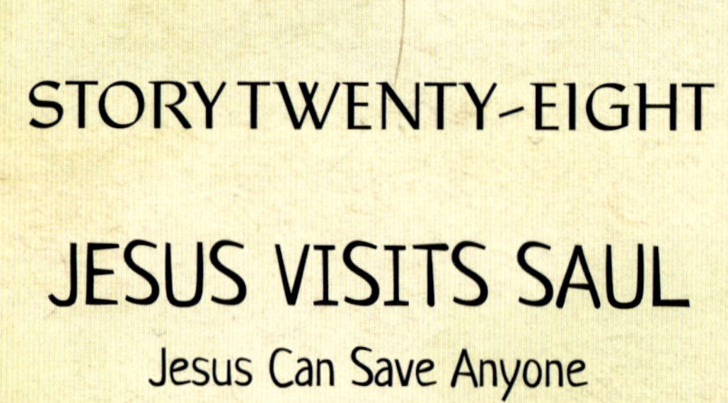

STORY TWENTY-EIGHT

JESUS VISITS SAUL

Jesus Can Save Anyone

(ACTS 9)

Who are some of your friends? How did you make those friends? Making friends can be easy if we like the same things, like the same games or foods or jokes. But it can also be difficult sometimes. What if people don't like what we do? Or what if they're mean to us? One of my favorite things about Jesus is that he wants to be friends with everyone. This story shows us that anyone can become Jesus's friend, even someone who used to hurt God's people.

THE LIGHT OF THE WORLD

After the three thousand people believed in Jesus and were baptized, they spread out and told everyone they knew about Jesus. I marveled at how many people decided to follow Jesus. We met together often to share stories about Jesus and explain his teaching. Everyone leaned in close to listen. We obeyed all of the commandments Jesus had taught. Whenever someone needed food or clothes or a place to stay, we took care of each other. We'd pray together and sing songs and share meals. We called this regular gathering the church.

You might have heard about the church before. The church is the people of God, people we call Christians. Sometimes Christians meet in big, beautiful buildings, sometimes they meet in homes, sometimes under a tall, shady tree. But all Christians love Jesus, have his Holy Spirit, and obey Jesus' teaching. They serve people in a way that shows others the light and love of Jesus.

Jesus once told us that his followers were "the light of the world—like a city on a hilltop that cannot be hidden." Jesus shines his light through us, like a candle in a dark room or a lit-up city at night. When we help someone in need or share our things with others, it's like we're glowing. Our good deeds sparkle and shine, and others get to see what Jesus is like.

MEAN PEOPLE HURT THE CHURCH

The church twinkled like stars, but some mean people didn't like it. They felt threatened by the Christians because they kept saying, "Jesus is King!" To the mean people, Jesus wasn't the king; Caesar was. So they attacked the Christians and told them, "Be quiet! Stop telling everyone that Jesus is King, or we'll throw you in prison."

When the mean people told me and Peter to stop talking about Jesus, we said, "Do you think God wants us to obey you rather than him? We cannot stop telling about everything we have seen and heard." We'd seen Jesus with our eyes. We knew he was alive. We had to tell everyone the good news, no matter what. And that made the mean people really, really angry. They threw us in prison and started persecuting the church.

Persecution is a big word, isn't it? It's what happens when people who don't love God get really angry at Christians for talking about and acting like Jesus, so they hurt them. Persecution sounds scary, and it can be. But remember, Jesus loves us. He takes care of us. So even if mean people hurt us, we can trust that everything true about Jesus never changes. Christians always shine Jesus' light to the world, even if other people are mean to them.

SAUL MEETS JESUS

A man named Saul hated Jesus and all the people who followed him. He took charge of the persecution of the church by making sure Christians ended up in prison or hurt because they loved Jesus. Anger rumbled in his heart, and he came up with an evil plan. He would go to a town called Damascus and recruit other angry people to help him arrest and hurt Christians.

He set out on the road, eager to enact his evil plan. *I'll make sure every Christian goes to prison,* he thought.

Suddenly, a bright light flashed all around him like lightning. He squinted and tried to see where the light came from. A voice boomed, "Saul! Saul! Why are you persecuting me?"

Who could it be? Were the Christians playing a trick on him? "Who are you? Show yourself!" exclaimed Saul.

"I am Jesus, the one you are persecuting! Now get up and go into the city, and you will be told what you must do."

Jesus flashed away, and all fell quiet. Saul blinked, trying to get his eyes to adjust back to the normal light of day. But he couldn't see—not a single thing. Jesus had blinded him. How do you think Saul felt? He'd just met Jesus, and he'd said Saul was hurting *him.* What could this mean?

You see, Jesus loves his people so much that when they are in pain, he hurts too. It's like when a friend has a bad day and you feel sad for them. So when Saul harmed Christians, Jesus was hurt too.

Saul had met Jesus, the Light of the World, and Jesus had given him something to do. So he went up to the city, just as Jesus had told him.

There, he met a man named Ananias. Jesus had appeared to Ananias in a dream, telling him to help Saul. But Ananias was confused—Saul harmed Christians. Why would Jesus want Ananias to help Saul?

Jesus told him, "I have an important mission for Saul. He's going to go all over the world and tell people about me."

So Ananias found Saul and prayed that he'd be healed, and he was. Immediately, Saul believed in Jesus and got baptized.

GOD'S PLAN FOR SAUL

Jesus changed Saul's name to Paul, and Paul followed God's mission for him. God's biggest enemy became God's missionary. A missionary is someone who tells others about Jesus wherever they go. Paul went all over the world, telling everyone about Jesus.

Mean people didn't like Paul's message, so they threw him in prison, hurt him, and said unkind things to him. But guess what Paul did? He loved them! He followed Jesus' teaching, "Love your enemies! Pray for those who persecute you!" Often, when he was in prison, he'd write letters to other Christians, encouraging them to keep following Jesus. And we still have those letters in the New Testament. Because of Paul, the good news spread everywhere.

John Reflects

Paul's story shows us that Jesus can save anyone. Even Jesus' enemies can become his friends. And Jesus wants to be friends with everyone. We get to help people become Jesus' friend by telling them the story of Jesus and showing them his love. **Jesus shines his light through us, so let's be like Paul and tell everyone the good news about Jesus.**

THE LIGHT MOMENT

Jesus' followers are the light of the world, because Jesus shines his light through us, even when we're persecuted. Saul met Jesus as he was traveling, and he went from persecuting other Christians to proclaiming Jesus, the Light. Like Paul, let's tell everyone the good news.

Questions for Conversation

What's something you can do to shine the light of Jesus?

Who is someone you want to help become Jesus' friend?

Prayer

Jesus, you are the Light of the World, and you shine your light through me. I pray for my friend who doesn't know you. I pray they'll become your friend. Amen.

STORY TWENTY-NINE

WALKING IN THE LIGHT

God Makes Us More like Jesus Through the Spirit

(1 JOHN 1–5)

Did you know I wrote several books? One is about my time with Jesus on the earth; three others are about how to live our lives because of how Jesus lived his; and the last one is about the end of the age. You'll learn about that last book in the next story.

Today, I'm pulling from the second book I wrote—about how to live out what Jesus taught us. **He constantly warned us about darkness and told us to walk in the light.** I want to help you walk in the light too.

RETELLING THE STORY

I only write all this down because I've seen the whole story of Jesus. To talk about what you have seen is called testifying. Like in a courtroom, when someone gives a testimony about what the truth is—they are called witnesses.

As a witness to the life of Jesus, I spent three glorious years with him. I watched him heal people with diseases—legs strengthened, eyesight recovered, bleeding stopped, hearing given back, crippled limbs restored, leprosy completely healed—all miraculous. I watched as he cast out angry demons. I heard him teach us how to pray. I drank wine that should have been water. I witnessed thousands of people eat a meal made up of five small loaves of simple bread and two bony fish—and there were leftovers. I saw Jesus turn a storm into the stillest of waters. I hugged Lazarus after Jesus had raised him back to life.

I especially noticed how angry our religious leaders became throughout Jesus' adult life, how at every turn, they'd question, belittle, and harass Jesus. I knew they wanted him gone. Their hatred spoiled everything, and I could feel the doom in my chest. This wouldn't end well.

Especially after the miracle of Lazarus—that's when everything sped up. And as we ventured back into Jerusalem for Passover, I had a sinking feeling.

For a moment, there was joy. When Jesus entered the capital city with triumph and people waved palm branches and threw their coats down before Jesus as he rode regally on a donkey, I felt like maybe everything would turn out well. "Hosanna," they sang. But their praises wouldn't last. *Perhaps*, they thought, *Jesus will be our king and get rid of Rome and all their terrible rules and soldiers and leaders.*

But that did not happen.

Jesus expelled our people making money in the Temple—not the Romans.

We dined on a strange Passover meal where Jesus washed our feet and charged us to serve others in the same way. Then he told us someone would betray him, someone we later found out was Judas Iscariot. Judas had been my friend. He betrayed us all.

I saw the agony in the garden, the sweat of Jesus' brow weeping like blood down his forehead, and I heard his cries as he chose to do the will of his Father. He chose the cross. He obeyed.

The arrest. The fake trial. The weakness of Pilate. The screaming of the leaders and the crowd to crucify Jesus.

The pierced wrists and ankles.

The crown of thorns upon his head.

People snatching his clothes beneath him.

The three crosses, Jesus between thieves, though he was innocent.

Blood that ran down, wetting the earth below.

Jesus forgiving those who crucified him.

Him giving me a new family in his mother.

Jesus hanging his head as the world darkened, then blackened.

His burial in the cave with the rolled stone.

The silence of the Sabbath. Did the birds even chirp?

And then?

The stone rolled away.

Jesus rising from the dead on that third day, Sunday.

The women witnessing the miracle, mouths open, eyes wide.

He appeared to me. I am a witness to this.

He appeared to hundreds.

He walked dusty paths, ate meals, and shared about the coming Kingdom.

On day forty in his resurrected body, he flew to heaven like a dove on a mission.

And ten days later, he sent us the dove back—as the Holy Spirit—prompting the beginning of the church of God's people.

HOW TO LIVE

I share these things because I want you to know what I saw, what I felt, and what I experienced. But I mainly share them so that your joy would be the fullest it can be. You can't live fully if you're walking in darkness.

Remember when Jesus said he was the Light of the World?

In my book, I wrote, "God is light, and there is no darkness in him at all. So we are lying if we say we have fellowship with God but go on living in spiritual darkness; we are not practicing the truth." I think of my friend Judas, who seemed to live in the light, but whose life was one big lie.

But I wrote this as I thought about the remaining, faithful disciples. "But if we are living in the light, as God is in the light, then we have fellowship with each other, and the blood of Jesus, his Son, cleanses us from all sin."

That's what I want for you—to be cleansed. To make friends with Jesus's other friends. To live in the light. To be free from sin.

LOVE GOD; LOVE OTHERS

To live in the light, we simply need to look at Jesus' life. He spent a lot of time with his Father, learning what the Father wanted him to do. He honored his Father by choosing to face the cross for us. He showed that he loved the Father by obeying him.

It's the same for you. **You can show your love for the Father by obeying him.** I wrote, "If someone claims, 'I know God,' but doesn't obey God's commandments, that person is a liar and is not living in the truth. But those who obey God's word truly show how completely they love him. That is how we know we are living in him. Those who say they live in God should live their lives as Jesus did."

Remember when we talked about the Ten Commandments—that they were split into two parts? The first four commandments showed us how important it is to love God with everything inside us. And the last six commandments were about how we treat other people. Simply put, we're to love God and love others. If you ever get confused about how to live a life as a Jesus follower, just remember those two things.

If we hate someone else, we show we're not really following Jesus, who died for everyone—including those who hated him.

There's a way I like to think about it. Love equals light. Hate equals dark.

I put it simply in my book: "But anyone who hates a fellow believer is still living and walking in darkness. Such a person does not know the way to go, having been blinded by the darkness."

If you want to be a light-walker, love needs to be your goal. And in order to love that way (oh, it's so hard), you need a Helper—the Holy Spirit of God—to empower you to forgive those who have hurt you, let go of the pain from the past, find ways to serve and love others (even the hard people to love), and love God with everything inside you.

John Reflects

The gospel is really quite simple. I wrote, "God showed us how much he loved us by sending his one and only Son into the world so that we might have eternal life through him. This is real love—not that we loved God, but that he loved us and sent his Son as a sacrifice to take away our sins." What good news! God didn't leave us alone on this earth as orphans, but he adopted us as his children. We no longer need to be afraid or worried. We no longer have to try to fix ourselves in our own strength. We have the Holy Spirit inside us to help us love God and love others. Such a gift!

You already have life—eternal, beautiful, joyful life—because of what Jesus did for us on the cross, and through the power and truth of his resurrection. I wrote, God "has given us eternal life, and this life is in his Son. Whoever has the Son has life; whoever does not have God's Son does not have life." You, my friend, have the light and the life.

Now take that light to the darkened world.

THE LIGHT MOMENT

Jesus sent us the Holy Spirit to live in us and be our Helper. He also warned us about darkness and told us to walk in the light. We show our love for the Father when we obey his commands and when we love others.

Questions for Conversation

Why do you think John likens sin to darkness? And love and truth to light? How do you feel when you're hurting God with your actions? Or other people? How do you feel when you "come clean" and confess your sins to others? What happens?

In your own words, with the help of John's words, share the gospel. What does it mean?

Prayer

Jesus, I don't want to walk in darkness. I want to love you and love others. Please send your Holy Spirit and teach me to walk in the light. Amen.

STORY THIRTY

THERE WILL BE NO MORE DARKNESS

Someday, God Will Always Be Our Light

(REVELATION 1, 21)

Every story has an ending, right? This big story has an ending too—kind of. **The ending of the Bible is also the beginning of a beautiful forever story.** I know that might sound confusing. It confused me, too, which is why Jesus helped me understand a little bit better. And now I get to share what he told me with you.

A SPECIAL DREAM

I wrote my last book because Jesus gave me a special dream all about our happy future with God. The dream started with Jesus, but he looked different from the last time I had seen him floating to the sky. He glowed like a star, his voice boomed like a thunderclap, and he wore a glimmering royal robe. He was so bright and amazing that he took my breath away. I fell down at his feet to worship him.

He said, "Don't be afraid! I am the First and the Last. I am the Living One. I died, but look—I am alive forever and ever!"

Why do you think Jesus said he was the First and the Last? It's because he's God. He's always been around. At the very beginning, he created the world. And at the very end, he'll be there too. He's alive forever and ever. He's the beginning and the end of the story. He's the King.

When I had the special dream, all of the Christians, including me, needed to remember that Jesus is the King. You see, it had been years and years since Jesus had floated into heaven. We'd thought he'd come back soon, but he still hadn't returned yet. We'd waited and waited. And while we'd waited, things had gotten really difficult. Some Christians had been thrown in prison, some hurt by mean people, and some even killed because they'd loved Jesus. We needed our good King Jesus to come back and help us.

JESUS IS KING

When I saw Jesus all shining and shimmering, my heart filled with hope. Jesus, the King, must have a plan to rescue us once and for all! As the rest of the special dream unfolded, I got to see parts of his plan. A lot of it didn't make sense to me, but there are three things I know for sure. The first we've already talked about: Jesus is the King. No one can take him off his throne. He rules forever and ever, and he's the most powerful in the whole universe.

What kind of a king is Jesus? He's kind. He's full of love and grace. He's also powerful and mighty, able to defeat any enemy. And he's just—that means he won't let evil win. **In my dream, I saw Jesus in the throne room of heaven. He was ready to rescue his people from all the evil in the world.**

JESUS WINS!

That brings me to the second important thing I learned in the special dream. Jesus wins. Remember back in the very good garden of Eden? The sneaky snake, Satan, convinced Adam and Eve to eat the forbidden fruit, and sin and death entered the world. But God promised a Rescuer would come, and the Rescuer would squish the sneaky snake. Jesus had already solved the problem of sin and death when he came, died, and rose again. But the sneaky snake still roamed the earth doing evil things everywhere he went.

In my special dream, I saw the sneaky snake. But he had grown into a huge dragon with claws and wings and sharp teeth. He did cruel, horrible things to God's people and the whole world. Christians from everywhere in the world cried out to God for help.

God had enough of his people's suffering. So Jesus came galloping on a horse with anger flashing in his eyes. He returned to squish the sneaky snake! Do you think he succeeded? Of course he did! He's Jesus, after all. Without much effort, because he's the most powerful in the whole universe, he won the battle!

Now remember, this all happened in my special dream. That means it hasn't happened just yet. But my special dream is also a promise. And what's true about God's promises? They always come true. **Someday, Jesus will come back to us and destroy the sneaky snake for good.** When we feel sad or confused or afraid, we can remember who wins. It's Jesus! We follow the God who is stronger than anyone or anything. And he always keeps his promises. We can trust him.

OUR HAPPY FUTURE WITH GOD

And guess what? There's one more thing I learned from my special dream—another promise. God has a happy future planned out for us. In this happy future, no one will ever shed a tear again. We won't have pain or fear or stress. Little kids can be friends with lions and lambs. God will make the world brand-new, just like it was in the very beginning. We'll be with all God's people forever—people who look and sound different than us but who all love Jesus. And most important of all, we'll be with God. **He'll live with us and shine so bright that we won't even need the sun anymore.** Here's what I heard in my dream:

"Look, God's home is now among his people! He will live with them, and they will be his people. God himself will be with them. He will wipe every tear from their eyes, and there will be no more death or sorrow or crying or pain. All these things are gone forever."

I saw the place God is preparing for us too. It's amazing! A glowing city with a river and a garden like the one he made in the beginning. Imagine it with me. Picture a place where you never get sad, where you never see darkness again, and where you get to hang out with Jesus all the time. You'll laugh and play and create and dance and sing songs with Jesus. Doesn't that sound like fun? I can't wait to be in our happy place forever with Jesus.

John Reflects

We've come to the end of this story, but remember, it's only the beginning of our story. Jesus is our King who rules forever and ever. He will return to rescue us from the sneaky snake forever. And he has a happy future planned for us. His promises always come true. We can trust that everything in my special dream will happen someday because God promised it would. In the meantime, what should we do? We keep following Jesus, the Light of the World, who shines through us into a dark world.

THE LIGHT MOMENT

The ending of the Bible is also the beginning of a beautiful forever story. Jesus is in the throne room of heaven, ready to rescue his people. Someday, he will come back to us and destroy Satan for good. Then God will live with us and shine so bright we won't even need the sun anymore.

Questions for Conversation

Are you glad Jesus will destroy the sneaky snake?
How does the ending of the story make you feel?

What do you think our happy future with Jesus will be like? What are you most looking forward to? What will it be like to always be in the light with God?

Prayer

Jesus, you are the King, and you are more powerful than anyone. Thank you that you will come back someday and defeat the sneaky snake, Satan. I am excited to spend my forever future with you. Amen.

CONCLUSION

SHINE THE LIGHT

Believe and Share God's Story

(JOHN 12:46)

We've finished God's big story, and what have we found? We saw God's light shining everywhere. From the moment God said, "Let there be light," to the end when he will shine as our light in our happy future with him, God always has been and always will be flooding the world with his light. Even when it seemed like darkness was winning, God's light burst through.

And we witnessed the best way God's light shone bright. In our complete darkness, Jesus came to us. He's the Light of the World, our Rescuer. He came to save us from sin and death and to squish the sneaky snake, Satan. He lived perfectly, performed many miracles, and taught us about God. Then he died. But he didn't stay dead, did he? Jesus is alive! He's in heaven now, waiting for the day he will come back and defeat the sneaky snake once and for all. Then, we'll all enjoy our happy future with him.

In this story, we also learned about faith. Since the beginning, God's people have had faith—they believed in something they couldn't see. And their faith made them move. They obeyed God, even when what he asked seemed crazy or silly. They believed the promises God made to them, and they followed his lead. This story showed us that all of God's promises will come true no matter what. We can trust God.

We have a choice to make, now that we know the story. Will we have faith in God, or not? I cannot ignore what I have seen and heard from Jesus—can you? I want to be like Noah and Abraham, Ruth and Mary, David and Paul, people who all put their faith in God. I hope you do too. If you do, you can pray this prayer:

Jesus, You died upon a cross
And rose again to save the lost
Forgive me now of all my sin
Come be my Savior, Lord, and Friend
Change my life and make it new
And help me, Lord, to live for You

If you believe in Jesus, hooray! That means the Holy Spirit lives in you. He shines the light of Jesus through your words and actions so others can see what Jesus is like. You're part of God's big family, the church, and you will live with God forever in the happy future he has planned for us.

Thanks for joining me on this journey through the story of the Light of the World. I want to end with these words from Jesus that you can share with others and say to yourself to remember the story. He said, "I have come as a light to shine in this dark world, so that all who put their trust in me will no longer remain in the dark." I hope you will tell this story to your friends and family. Let's all shine the light of Jesus wherever we go!

ABOUT THE AUTHORS

Mary DeMuth is a literary agent, daily podcaster at *Pray Every Day*, Scripture artist, speaker, and the author of over fifty books, including *Around the Word in 60 Seconds: The Ultimate Tween Devotional* (Tyndale). She lives in Texas with her husband and is mom to three adult children, including coauthor Sophie. Find out more at marydemuth.com.

Sophie DeMuth is a writer, editor, and publisher at RightNow Media. She's the author of *Light of the World: Josiah's Story*. She lives in Dallas, Texas.

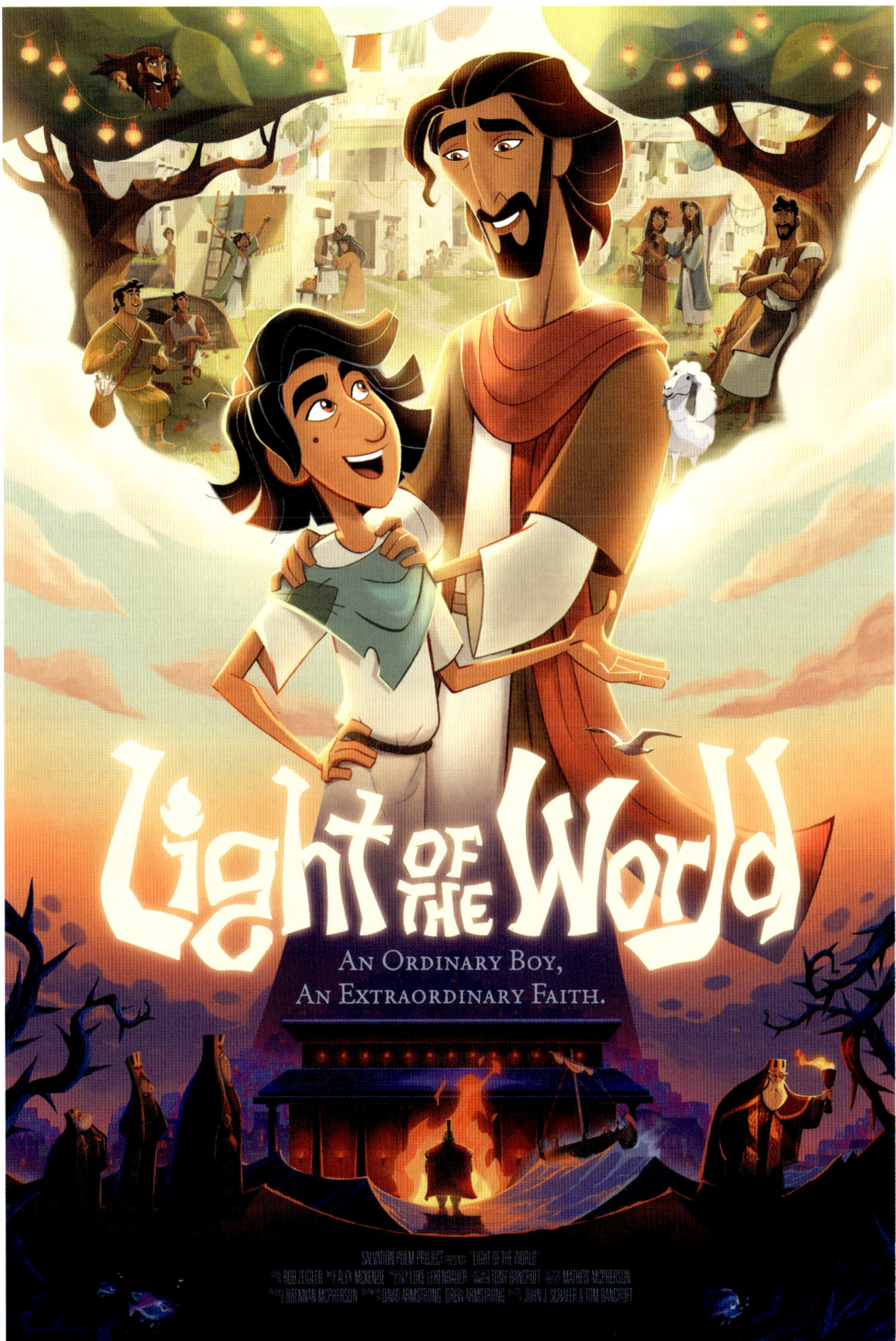
Light of the World
An Ordinary Boy,
An Extraordinary Faith.
SALVATION POEM PROJECT "LIGHT OF THE WORLD"
ROB ZEIGLER ALEX MCKENZIE LUKE LEHENBAUER TONY BANCROFT MATHEW MCPHERSON
BRENNAN MCPHERSON DAVID ARMSTRONG DREW ARMSTRONG JOHN J. SCHAFER & TOM BANCROFT

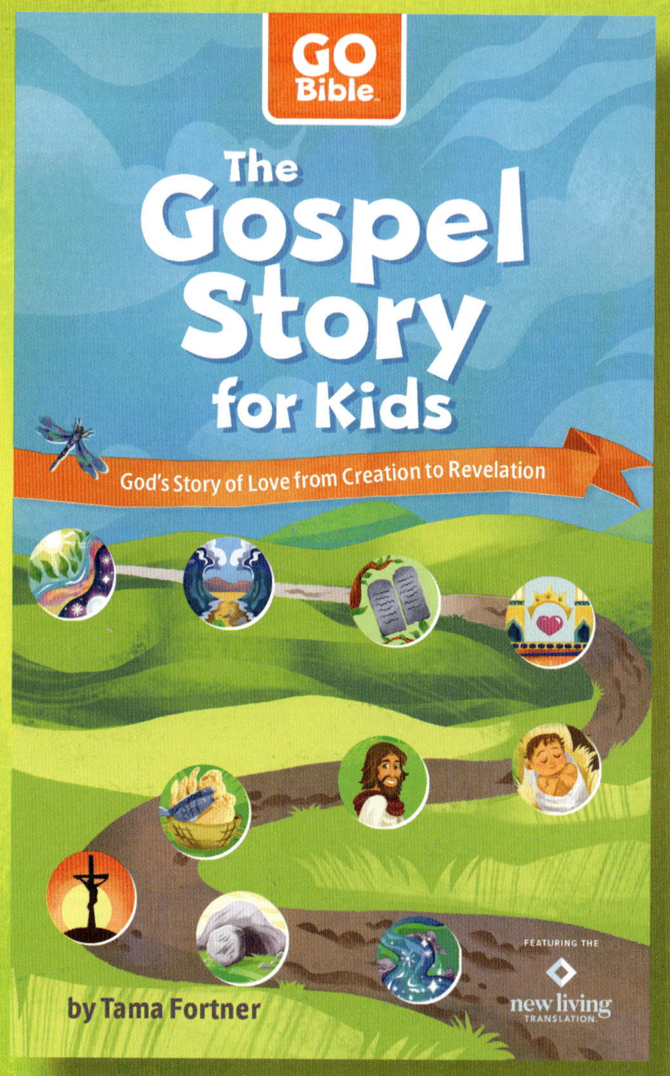
GO
Bible
The Gospel Story for Kids
God's Story of Love from Creation to Revelation
FEATURING THE
new living
TRANSLATION
by Tama Fortner